Hard Days' Journey into Night

ii

Hard Days' Journey into Night

Memoirs of an MND warrior and human rights campaigner.

Noel D Conway

Dedication

As always I could not have produced this work without considerable help from my wife Carol whose support and patience have been superhuman at times. My good friend, Crispin Barker, has also been extremely generous with his time and invaluable advice in the proofreading and editing stages. Particular thanks are given to Davina, Ellie and Tom at Dignity in Dying who have patiently checked and where necessary corrected legal references and arguments. Another group of people whom I have come to rely on more and more, and without whom this task would not be possible, are my wonderful caring team: Anita, Camilla, Fiona, Kimberley, Louise, Sarah and not forgetting the management team at Home Instead: Caroline, Holly and Rachael.

Noel and Carol in July 2015

Table of Contents

Introduction

I am a 68 year old, white male who in November 2014 was diagnosed with Motor Neurone Disease (MND). It is a muscle wasting disease that is terminal with no cure at present and for which life expectation is from 2 to 5 years after diagnosis. Unremarkably, my life and that of my family has undergone a profound change in the last four years. We have all had to adapt to frightening and challenging circumstances made worse by not knowing when the end will come. There are a number of reasons why I wanted to make this record, which I never expected to do, since I am not famous nor a celebrity except by way of the publicity I have received during the last 18 months.

Firstly, as an MND sufferer I know how little information there is for others with the same condition and I wanted to provide some kind of road map as to what may happen to them. This is because the disease is so varied and its path so different from individual to individual. In the early days after my diagnosis, I scoured the Internet looking for just such personal accounts to give me more insight in an attempt to relieve the anxiety which I was feeling. Everything helped though I knew that it wasn't necessarily the course I would take. So, I hope there may be some comfort to others in these memoirs who are at the beginning of their journey. For that reason, I have provided information which may seem unusually detailed, especially in chapter five.

A second reason for this account is to leave a legacy for my family so that in later years they may return to it in order to understand who I was and what I was trying to do.

Another extremely important reason for this memoir, however, is to provide a platform for the campaign to improve Human Rights in the UK, so that everyone facing their final days will have the choice of an assisted death before them. I would hope, though it is a rather forlorn one, that I would be able to do the same but I don't think the law will be changed in time for me.

Before I retired, and in the few years leading up to it, having longed for the freedom which retirement offers, I found for the first time in my life I could not see any future. This was well before I was experiencing any symptoms of disease. I knew of course that I would look forward to making those long-distance Alpine treks allowing me to delve more deeply into the history, culture and language of the Europe I love; to travel the coastal paths of my own dear country; to ski and cycle; and to travel to those parts of the world which I have not yet explored, such as the USA, Central America, Japan and New Zealand, the country of my early childhood. But I knew there needed to be more and these excursions would soon become wearisome unless there was something more meaningful. Then I could not see it, but now I do, and ironically it is a result of MND.

As will become clear later in this book, what I am seeking is legal recognition for a process of assisted dying. I cannot emphasise too much that this is not euthanasia, which is when someone else, such as a doctor, administers a lethal concoction directly to a person. It is not to be confused with the withdrawal of treatment because it is an action intended to end someone's life, albeit for compassionate reasons. Assisted dying, however, is when the person who wishes to die is fully conscious and actively administers a lethal mixture to themselves. Currently this is not possible in the UK, unless one travels to Switzerland to make use of the services of Dignitas. However, the latter course is not without problems as it runs the risk of a criminal investigation to assess the motives behind assisting someone to die. Consequently, many thousands of people in the UK, often with incurable cancers, face the very real likelihood of unmitigated suffering at the end-of-life. This should not be necessary, nor inevitable, as other countries have shown and, as I argue, is a denial of the individual's human rights, to choose the manner and method of their own death.

I am, therefore, currently engaged in a legal suit against the British Government[1] that the Suicide Act 1961 should be amended. The provisions of an amended Act would allow terminally ill people to die painlessly and peacefully in their own homes. There should be safeguards so that weak and vulnerable people are not coerced into doing something they don't want. My legal team and the campaign group with whom I am working, Dignity in Dying, have specified that it should only apply to terminally ill people with less than six months to live. Furthermore, two doctors should confirm the individual is terminal and of sound mind. Finally, it will be necessary for a High Court judge to ensure he or she is not subject to immoral or criminal influence, and, having satisfied all the above conditions, has the right to end their lives with the help of a physician by the provision of a lethal drug. This is nothing less than what we are entitled to as a human right as enshrined in Article 8 of the European Convention on Human Rights (1998). To date, a number of legal hurdles have been overcome and I and my legal team are awaiting an Appeals Court judgement towards the end of July. Whatever the outcome, the legal and political importance of this case will ensure that the final step will be in the Supreme Court, but it will be for Parliament in the end to draw up the details of any new legislation.

Win or lose, this issue will not go away and it is just a matter of time before the UK passes suitable legislation that is compassionate, safe and in response to the wishes of the majority of the population.

Noel D Conway
July 2018

Chapter 1

First Signs

Madeira

Madeira looks like the splash of an artist's palette in early summer. It was thrilling to be leaving the grey skies of the UK behind to head due south into the Atlantic towards the Tropic of Cancer. For Carol and I until now our holidays had been confined to Europe, where we spent much of our time cycling and walking in the Austrian Alps and the Salzkammergut, famous for its warm water lakes.

This is a popular destination for many retired people from northern Europe and one can understand why with its constant daily temperatures of 25°C. As the small Boeing aeroplane dipped and turned on its descent to the island, we could clearly see the landing strip protruding alarmingly out into the sea. As we took in the view, we saw that the island is extremely mountainous consisting of great ridges and ravines running down to the coast. Apart from the recently constructed motorway on the south of the island, there is hardly a straight road for more than a hundred metres anywhere, even in the capital, Funchal.

Carol and I had done our homework. We bought maps of the island and studied the websites closely, so we knew there were some excellent high-level routes to cross. We were especially keen to explore a famous feature of Madeira, the lavados. These date back 600 years in some instances and are ingenious irrigation channels installed by the early settlers to provide fresh water to the settlements in the ravines, on the coast and in the capital. The lavados are a wonder of engineering maintaining continuously declining irrigation channels, for 50 miles in some cases, boring directly through mountain sides and zigzagging down with their precious contents to the populations below. Today, it has become a popular and enjoyable activity to walk these routes, which can be dangerously precipitous on one side without the security of iron railings or hand cables. This all adds to the allure and excitement for the intrepid, mountain walker that we considered ourselves to be. On the first day, we drove our little hire car up the endlessly snaking, narrow roads to the highest point of the island, Pico Ruivo, over 6000 feet above sea level. Carefully avoiding the many roadworks, made necessary by violent mudslides last year, we finally arrived at the summit emerging through an inversion of dense mist, caused by Atlantic precipitation. We arrived in brilliant sunshine where the ambient temperature was around 30° C. The plan was to follow a steep trail to a mountain Pueblo below, from which we knew we could catch a bus to return us back up the mountain to where we had parked.

It was during that descent that I began to struggle with my knees and hips. I had taken to using a pair of walking poles some years before, and these became my lifeline because without them I could not have completed the trek. Once on the level, I could walk normally again and, apart from the odd twinge, I thought nothing more about it.

We thoroughly enjoyed our time in Madeira, and in spite of the altitude and numerous stairways encountered, were able to complete one of the highest routes in the whole island. We dived into the murky Atlantic from a replica galleon and climbed back on-board spitting out stinging salt water. We feasted and drank well in our quinto apartment beneath our own special banana tree. What a glorious time! We looked forward to returning to the island to explore more of it in the future, but that was never to happen.

Corfu

The following year we decided to visit a Greek island, Corfu. Some years before, we had enjoyed a great week in Zante with our son, Alex, hiring scooters and travelling all over the island. This time we were on our own as Alex preferred to do his own thing. We researched the best place for us, identifying a quiet resort in the north-west of the island, Santa Georgio. It turned out to be the perfect location. It was only a week, but that was often enough for us when it concerned a small island, sea and sun. This time it was the exception, when we would cheerfully have stayed longer. The heat was more intense than in Madeira but not unbearable. We were lucky enough to have found a cool, though spartan apartment that was scrupulously swept every day. It belonged to a small, local setup of apartments with a sparkling swimming pool and a family-run bar/restaurant. Each evening we enjoyed strolling down the hill to the many other competing restaurants in the little community providing excellent food and drink. It was wonderful walking along the varied coastline, some of which rose steeply to clifftops where we could gaze out to the small islands and order a delicious cup of Greek coffee from one of the many small bars that dotted the area.

It was whilst climbing up one of the steep cliffs that Carol first noticed I seemed to be breathing shallowly. When she mentioned it, I became aware of it myself and thought the extra drink and cuisine must have been the cause. I made a mental note to go to the gym more frequently and get rid of the extra pounds that had accumulated around my waistline. When she mentioned again, however, that I was struggling going uphill, I was rather short with her and said it was nothing. I continued to walk up demanding cliff paths but always with the aid of walking poles and I realised, though I wouldn't have admitted it, that Carol found it easier and was climbing more strongly than I.

Back Pain

Finally, the time came when I had to accept that something wasn't quite right. We were in London, visiting my stepson and his girlfriend who lived in Walthamstow at the time. Often we would take the opportunity to explore central London, its eateries, museums and art galleries. Normally, we were able to walk around the city quite easily. On this occasion, after visiting the Greenwich Observatory and the Maritime Museum, we were on our way towards Covent Garden for a civilised cup of coffee and cake. It was at that moment, I became aware of a deep-seated ache and each step became a little more difficult to take causing me to rest continually. I then noticed that my ability to walk very far began to decline, so I got into the habit of taking my walking poles everywhere, even in the city centre. I must've looked a bit of a plonker.

Back pain afflicts millions of people around the world. It can be the result of poor posture or a harbinger of something much more sinister. Many people continue to live with it and carry on with their normal, daily lives. Indeed, quite recently a health report has said that for the vast majority suffering from back pain, the best advice is just to continue with an active life - the more active, the better. But that is not always the case nor is it always possible and so it was with me. The pain seemed to be located in the bottom right hand side of my back and it became so problematic that I found it too uncomfortable to sit on a normal sofa or chair. Eventually, I found the cleverly designed IKEA chairs to be the only ones I could use, to the extent of taking one on holiday with me. Fortunately, they dismantle and reassemble very easily. I also began to think about what other ways I could deal with this pain. I noticed that one of the Pilates' classes at the sports club I attended said it was especially good for reducing back pain, so I enrolled on it. I also increased my attendance at the gym and focused on strengthening my core muscles. I even bought a book on Tai Chi. On the days I didn't work, because now I was part-time, I spent quite a bit of time trying to master the intricacies of this ancient exercise. It wasn't easy and I have to confess I did give up. I think this was mainly because my ability to balance was already impaired by the insidious, almost unnoticeable, weakening of the core muscles. Carol and I still went for walks, but increasingly it was clear to both of us that I had real problems climbing hills. Each Monday, when I was not working, I set off from home to walk the 50 minutes it usually took me to climb to the top of the Wrekin behind our house. I loved to go up through the pine forest and take the steep scree slope to what is called Hell's Gate. It became a test of endurance and a marker of how much my strength was dwindling. I used to enjoy the return journey when I could walk normally again and almost run downhill. At no time during this year did I suspect that I would permanently lose my ability to walk. I was convinced it was just a matter of time before either my muscles strengthened or, as I was reluctantly forced to do, to consult medical opinion and obtain the necessary treatment and cure. It's amazing how we humans deny reality in a perpetual cloud of deluded hope.

As I reflect now on that period of 4 to 5 years ago, there were both hilarious and poignant moments. There was the time, for instance, when I joined a Body Balance class which combines Pilates, Tai Chi and Yoga in a series of what is supposed to be fluid, fluent movements and balanced poises. Right from the start, I had trouble with a yoga posture, The Tree, where one has to balance on one leg and bring the other to rest on the opposite knee. I always fell over when it was on the right leg. Remarkably, I could manage the Tai Chi warrior moves with the invisible sweep of the sword, balancing on one leg and stretching out my arms and remaining leg, then rapidly reversing the position. However, the last time I ever attended the class coincided with a video recording of it because the tutor, who was a new instructor, was collecting evidence for assessment. By this time, my core muscles were obviously not functioning properly and were protruding so that my gut looked as though I was six months pregnant. Furthermore, my balance had virtually disappeared, but I was so determined to get through the moves I wobbled around like a Bobo doll looking ready to crash to the floor at any moment, which I finally did. The poor instructor just looked at me forlornly in complete amazement. I don't know if he ever did receive a pass for that class.

One consolation, or so I thought, was that each time I weighed myself on the gym scales, I had lost weight. It was sometime later when I noticed that the weight was dropping far too rapidly, as much as 4 to 5 pounds a week, that I knew I was in trouble. I distinctly remember the last time I attended the sports club. I had befriended another user about my age and we often had a chat as we showered and got dressed. The last time I saw him, I described some of the physical difficulties I was having in the classes and he looked very concerned. When I took my kit from the locker, I had a premonition that it was going to be for the last time, and it was.

Pelagia

One of the most painful events was when I had to accept that I would not be able to continue playing my cello. I had returned to playing the cello at 58 years of age, after having played it for four years at secondary school. I had begun like most people with the violin, but, whether it was because I was so atrocious or my legs were suitably long, the music teacher suggested I try the cello. I don't ever remember taking music exams but I do recall scratching away in the school orchestra at two events. I remember also having to practise and taking the cumbersome beast back home, which caused a number of difficulties from time to time. Some bus conductors would insist I pay a full fare because the instrument took up a whole seat space. Sometimes I just didn't have the money for the beast and me so I had to walk home, requiring a good 4 miles of lugging it with me. I must've been keen. I had to walk through some lower-income residential areas and there were occasions when I became a target of ribaldry as a result. Fortunately, it was nothing more than this and I steeled myself to ignore all insults and carry on at a steady pace. I found if I did this, I would avoid any outright confrontation that no doubt would have resulted in injury to me or damage to the instrument. I'm surprised I persisted with the cello for as long as I did because in those days I was using a school loaned instrument, which was basic, and had no fine tuning. It would very rapidly slip out of tune and I had to spend ages using a music fork to obtain any reasonable sound at all.

I suppose I returned to playing because I was approaching retirement age and I felt there were a few things I still wanted to do. In particular, I had this far too ambitious plan to play the Bach cello suites. After five years, I actually did fulfil that ambition, even though I had reached only level V in the Royal Society of Music exams. After that required concentrating on music theory. My aim was to play the instrument for pleasure, not to learn music theory. So, I agreed with my music teacher that would be our goal and I did actually begin to play the Bach cello suite in C major. For my 60th birthday, Carol found a shop which sold better quality instruments than the one I had been using so far. I had acquired this on eBay for £150 from China, sent via Hamburg. I must admit I was a bit anxious awaiting the delivery expecting it to arrive in splinters, but it didn't and I was amazed at how well packed it was in its cardboard package. I didn't want to lavish a lot of money on an expensive instrument until I knew that it wasn't just a flash in the pan and I was serious about learning to play again. After two years, I could confirm this was the case. However, when Carol said I should get a better quality instrument now for my birthday I was overjoyed. When I went down to the music shop with her, I could play very little from memory except scales but it was sufficient to determine which I should purchase. In the end, I acquired a new one, again from China, but this was conservatoire standard and cost £1250. I tried some older UK made ones costing £4000 and over but found, rather surprisingly, they didn't sound as good as the one from China.

Over the past few years, Carol and I have developed the rather peculiar practice of naming large consumer items, as if they are a member of the family. For example, our little runabout Peugeot 107 was always referred to as Pudgy. Generally, these rather affectionate names were applied to vehicles; everyday equipment that was frequently used. I hadn't christened my previous cello, but I felt the need to this time. Probably because of the cost. The name I chose was taken from a favourite book of mine: *Captain Corelli's Mandolin* by Louis de Bernieres. Pelagia is the chief female character in the book whose father, the local doctor, has ensured she has a good education at home. Besides being beautiful, intelligent and well educated, she has a loving, faithful and strong personality. So, Pelagia was the name I adopted for my cello. Some readers might like to read more deeply into the fact that the violin cello has a rather wonderful curvaceous shape, but I can assure them that so far as I know this was not the reason for the naming. Nevertheless, I became very fond of Pelagia and tried to make at least an hour or two available each day for her as I practised the different pieces and scales for each grade. I was very pleased with the progress I was making and enjoyed the mellow sound which was possible to produce on this wonderful instrument, my Pelagia.

In November 2013, I began to experience difficulties in finding the right posture with Pelagia. I searched the Internet for advice and discussed the problem with my music teacher, who advised me to obtain a wedge-shaped cushion, which I did. It didn't seem to make much difference and after a while playing I would become fatigued and experience a slight lower backache, which by now was becoming too familiar. However, I persisted with various arrangements of pillows and cushions until a further development shattered my concert playing ambitions totally. In February 2014, I noticed the little finger on my right hand was becoming difficult to control. Now, it may not seem terribly important to a non-cellist but the little finger is absolutely crucial for stabilising the holding and playing of the bow. The consequence of this was that my bow began to slip and slide all over the strings in various directions, which made it impossible to play anything. At this time, I still didn't think it was anything particularly serious and, as I had already been referred to a medical consultant, I was confident that it was merely a matter of time before everything would be corrected and I could return to my lessons and my beloved Pelagia. In the first year after my diagnosis, I found it extremely emotional to listen to cello music, especially that which I'd been able to play myself such as the Swan by Saint Saens.

The Gower

In July 2014, Carol and I decided to revisit a spot we hadn't been back to in 30 years, the Gower Peninsula in south Wales. We had spent a fortnight exploring Pembrokeshire 30 years ago and had made a fleeting visit to the Gower Peninsular - a beautiful memory of an outstanding profile of jagged coastline in the UK. We had diligently located Dylan Thomas's writing shack, a poignant shrine to his genius. I had also the refreshing experience of urinating in the same stall as he did, no doubt many times, in Brown's Hotel. We had left it rather late to make a booking directly on the Gower but we did find what appeared to be suitable accommodation in the Mumbles adjacent to Swansea. We had thrown the bikes on the back of the car and set off in hopeful expectation of a wonderful reunion with this remarkably unique area of Wales. Swansea Bay has been completely refurbished and redesigned and there is a lovely cycle path all the way along it which enabled us to cycle from where we were staying in the Mumbles to the Dylan Thomas Centre by the city's Marina. It was a great route with a wonderful view and many places where we could stop and munch our sandwiches. The cycle route itself is mainly flat apart from where it rises slightly at the end where the lifeboat station is. I thought I noticed a slight difficulty going up these gradients. It was particularly pronounced on a one in three section that rises up to a viewing point. I had no option but to dismount and push the bike up with some effort. By now I had got used to the fact that hills, however small, could present me with a significant obstacle. Nevertheless, cycling along Swansea Bay was not arduous and one of the more pleasurable moments in our short holiday.

The following day was a gloriously sunny one at the Mumbles so we decided to explore the Gower Peninsula towards the west. The roads were swarming with frantic tourists on this summer bank holiday weekend but we were determined to enjoy a picnic on the beach. We had packed our walking poles so we could get down to the sea. Carol wanted to plunge into the welcoming waves, whilst I delved deeper into a history of the Plantagenets that I was currently enjoying. Given the difficulties I had walking uphill, our plans were not too ambitious and we headed for an attractive little sandy bay with a few rock outcrops here and there. The Damascene shock occurred when I tried to climb on one of these rocky prominences and found my legs wouldn't respond to my wishes. It was as if they were encased in a diving suit with heavy weights holding me to the bottom of the sea. I simply couldn't get my legs to respond at all. It was a dramatic and life changing event. One I could not possibly ignore. I would have to go back to my GP and insist that more effective investigations were carried out. A week later, I had an appointment with my GP, or rather, at the GP Practice, since I never seemed to see the same doctor each time. It was someone I hadn't met before, a new part-time doctor who listened attentively and compassionately. He agreed with me that it was high time to get to the bottom of this mystery and tackle the systematic obstacles that the NHS was placing in my way in order to receive an accurate diagnosis. At last, someone seemed to be taking my problems seriously, not the least of whom was me!

Chapter 2

First Stage of my MND Journey

Diagnosis

After six months waiting for an appointment with a neurologist at the local hospital, my new GP said he would arrange for one out of district in Sandwell. Why did it take so long? I have since discovered there is a desperate shortage of neurologists in the county and a reliable source has said there should be at least two more at the hospital by UK NHS standards [2]. This is still woefully inadequate when compared with European countries like France where the same size hospital and population would have at least 14. When one considers that there is an increasing number of neurological conditions affecting the population, it is hardly surprising that considerable delays in appointments are being experienced. Neurological illnesses are infamously difficult to diagnose and the extra suffering, as a result of delays because of understaffing, borders on the inhumane. Is this another health crisis time bomb waiting to go off?

I was able to drive myself to the appointment and went unaccompanied. I didn't see why I needed someone with me, but every visit after that my wife, Carol, was there to share my growing anxiety. It is remarkable how much we take for granted like the ability to travel independently, something that I cannot do at all now. This was the start of an insidious decline into dependency, which gradually erodes one's sense of self and status. I remember sitting in the waiting area momentarily noticing an elderly lady in a wheelchair. I didn't for a moment see any parallel between us. I returned to my book and she at once disappeared from my mind. How could I know that within six months I would be in exactly the same position, having had a generation stolen from me.

Finally, the attending nurse signalled for me to enter the consultant's tiny office, made even smaller by the presence of a medical student scribbling notes. The neurologist was avuncular but noncommittal. He asked about recent symptoms, tested my reflexes and balance, and finished by simply saying he would be in touch. And that, was that. I drove

19

home feeling confident it would only be a matter of time before the source of my problems was identified and I could be cured.

Shortly after this, I was surprised by how quickly an appointment was made for me to have electrical tests at the Queen Elizabeth Hospital, Birmingham (QE). I had nerve conduction tests and an EMG, which was unexpectedly painful. The medical technician told me he would contact my neurologist within the week. I was left wondering why everything seemed to be speeding up so quickly after so much delay. It soon became clear. The neurologist phoned me on my mobile one inauspicious Friday morning as I was walking out of Morrison's supermarket. He said he wanted me to see a specialist as soon as possible, though he didn't identify the specialism. When I asked him whether it might be MND, he reluctantly confirmed that it could. Within days, I had an appointment with a consultant MND specialist at QE. His clinic was frantically busy and I was the last on the list. He spent about 50 minutes observing my muscle movements and listening to the account of my symptoms to date. In a quiet, dignified, professional manner that was almost deadpan, he confirmed what I had been dreading all along: MND/ALS. I became aware of a young nurse, who had been patiently observing the clinician's examination. It materialised that she was a specialist MND nurse, who was allocated as the link between me and the MND clinicians. From thereon I would be fast-tracked into whatever health services were needed. The consultant was anxious to refer me as quickly as possible to the breathing unit at the Royal Stoke University Hospital.

I shouted in my head, 'I know what I've got! That's not what I want to know. ' But instead, gripping Carol's hand, and in as

20

equally an academic manner as the doctor, meekly asked, 'How long have I got? ' I knew it was terminal. He looked at me for a moment, probably weighing up just how much information he should give, then said in that same deadpan tone as before,

'It is difficult to be exact, but it is likely to be between 6 to 18 months given your difficulties with breathing and walking. '

Both Carol and I were traumatised. I don't remember stumbling back to the car nor the return journey home. For the next three months, both of us were in a perpetual state of shock, prone to dissolving uncontrollably into heavy sobbing and streaming tears.

I felt then that I didn't want to wait to die. I wanted it to be all over with, there and then! The thought of a long, slow, progressive deterioration into immobility was not possible to accept. And it still isn't. What made it worse, was the not knowing when it was going to happen or precisely what was going to happen. A fear of the unknown is the worst fear of all.

But I was also angry, inconsolably, deeply angry. Why had this happened to me? I was just about to turn 65 looking forward to a long and active retirement. I was fit and active getting to the gym frequently and climbing weekly up the wooded slopes of the Wrekin, behind our home. I had always regulated my weight so my BMI was around 25, didn't smoke, drank reasonably and generally considered myself to be in good health. For months after diagnosis, I felt what I later came to see as an irrational anger towards my peers, and those older than me who were clearly overweight and unhealthy, but who nonetheless could enjoy walking around and participate freely in all the other taken for granted delights of life. Now, I was faced with a previously unimagined future. And, a very short one. In fact, I was left with very little hope at all at a time that should have been the beginning of a long and leisurely retirement. It was difficult for both Carol and I to see other couples of our age enjoying each other's company. It seemed like a door had been irrevocably slammed in our faces.

Holiday Mania

The weekend following our devastating diagnosis, we had a long-standing arrangement to meet with Richard and Barbara, two dear friends whom we had known for over 30 years. What should we do? We had yet to let family and friends know. The venue was in a lovely old Elizabethan manor house and we decided that the change of scenery would be therapeutic. We remembered that Barbara was a highly trained palliative care, hospice nurse who would be able to provide a great deal of useful information. I was desperate to talk to her regarding the intimate details of how a life ends. In those early days, I wanted as much knowledge as possible about dying. It was a way of preparing myself psychologically for what was to come. I had been told I could have as little as six months to live - everyday seemed as though it were the penultimate one. I couldn't possibly know then that I would still be alive nearly 4 years later with a thirst for life. At the time, I hobbled around Stratford-upon-Avon using my extra pair of legs, the Alpine walking poles that had been my close companions for so many years. The perspective of my surroundings changed utterly.

Taking advantage of a guided tour of the new and refurbished theatres in the Stratford Playhouse, I began to consider how accessible the seating would be for me and whether in future visiting the theatre would be possible in my gradually diminishing world. My lasting memory of that first weekend away living with our new terrible reality was Eva Cassidy's wonderful version of Fields of Gold. It made us both weep and still retains that power today.

A few weeks later on a visit to my daughter, Ashley, and her partner, Andy, I had my first real taste of what it was like to be disabled. A friendly neighbour, whose husband had died of MND a few years earlier, loaned us a manual wheelchair. Without it I would not have been able to get around the little, harbour town of Whitehaven.

Andy is an adept cook and, like most alpha males, takes every opportunity to barbecue. After a few beers, when my daughter had disappeared inside to restock the alcohol, I confided in him that I would not allow myself to deteriorate to a completely immobile and paraplegic state. I was still in shock and had a very bloody-minded attitude to what was happening to me. It would be a long time before I came to terms with the fact that I was disabled and terminal. I remember being pushed around Keswick and dining in the famous Dog and Gun public house. But, this experience was hardly more than dipping my toes in the ocean because I could still stand up and walk to the toilet, negotiating a few steps. I realised I would come to depend on the wheelchair increasingly. This thought began to penetrate my brain more and more despite me trying to push it aside. It was the first powerful psychological impact since my diagnosis and I had to recognise there would be more. I

23

became frustrated with the manual wheelchair because I could not control precisely where it went. I was left with little option but to rely on others, not something I was used to. I was already experiencing serious loss of upper arm strength so I needed something else other than a manual wheelchair - I needed a power chair and I was delighted when I got one six months later.

Just before Christmas was my birthday and the whole family got together to celebrate with my son and daughter staying over for a few days. It was on one of these days that an MND nurse from Queen Elizabeth's Hospital in Birmingham visited to provide more information and support. She said it was perfectly all right for my children to be present, but I wish they hadn't. I think she was probably rather inexperienced and consequently took insufficient notice of the impact of what she was saying on my children. She was far too forthcoming with details about the likely progression of the disease, especially about the end-of-life stage. My son was 22 years of age and my daughter 42 but they were both overcome by the raw emotion her description evoked. It was too cruel and I shouldn't have let it happen.

In the New Year , Carol encouraged me to think about what we could do in the near future. The MND literature advises sufferers and their carers to live one day at a time. For someone like me, this is very hard advice to take. I have always been a planner and thought well ahead about where I would be going and what I would be doing. But, as both Carol and I have discovered, such a philosophy limits one's horizons aspirations. That year we learned to plan one or two months ahead and took the view that if I was not well enough to travel, then we would simply lose the deposit already paid. I think that is still the best advice and would go further by saying that one's ambitions should not be limited by the illness. However, regrettably I think we have been guilty of ignoring this advice. Had we not, I think we could have done much more in that time. We were too quick to accept the prognosis of such a short period of time to live. Now, we are much more circumspect about accepting what doctors say. There were many other things that could have been done and places visited. For example, I would love to have travelled to the USA. I now realise that wouldn't have been impossible though it is now and was a year later.

London beckoned with its promise of a bucket list completed. Madame Butterfly at Covent Garden, Westminster Abbey, the Tate and the National Gallery awaited our attendance. There was a spectacular exhibition of Turner's works revealing the source of his inspiration from the classics which he believed he could better. Being disabled provided me with priority entrance and privileged viewing.

The London bus is an iconic image that we came to value increasingly each day during our stay. The Underground is a no-go area for the likes of me - its labyrinth of undulating passages, forbidden stairways and absent lifts have declared it out of bounds. Bright red and unmissable, the bus gave us free and unlimited access to wherever we wanted to go. The London Bus App connects 19th-century technology with the 21st, the live satellite feed able to pinpoint the traveller's position in real time. Expensive taxicab journeys are rendered redundant and there is the added bonus of actually being able to admire the city's architecture in place of fume filled Underground stations.

Nevertheless, there are some advantages with a taxi. The driver was a voluble source of information from Euston Station to Pimlico House, where we were staying. Without his help, we wouldn't have found the outstandingly authentic and welcoming Turkish restaurant in the centre of the village. Nor would we have had the delight of the promiscuous octogenarian couple who were racing towards the end of their lives by partying full-time as though they were permanently on speed.

A few weeks later and we were off again, this time in mid-February. Thrusting aside concerns about the weather, we zoomed off across country in search of East Anglia. I had always wanted to see this back corner of England, having only ever been there once on a honeymoon with my first wife. Now I wanted to share it with Carol by visiting Norwich Cathedral, King's Lynn and other places like Ely that still lingered in the memory. Experience had taught us not to rely on claims of good disabled accessibility, even from upmarket B&Bs, like the one we had booked into not too far from Cromer. We spent some time on the phone trying to establish that it was possible for my monstrous wheelchair to get into the building.We were assured it was. When we arrived, however, we were confronted by two immediate obstacles. The first was that the parking area was covered in Jurassic-sized pebbles in which any wheelchair rapidly sank and couldn't move. The prospect of my 135 kg power wheelchair negotiating this terrain was in the realm of the forlorn hope. Fortunately, Motability came to the rescue. We could reverse our wheelchair accessible vehicle up to the concrete perimeter around the house and thus deliver me onto hard ground. Such vehicles are essential equipment for power chair users but unless one is under 65 years of age, PIP (Personal Independence Payment) is unavailable and therefore must be purchased out of one's own pocket.

The struggle was not yet over. We still had to enter the property. There was a lip of 3 inches to surmount - beyond the limits of my otherwise reliable vehicle. The landlady had informed us that her husband had fashioned a little ramp to help with access. Unfortunately, when we inspected it, it was clearly too short to do the job. People don't realise that ramps need a shallow angle of no more than 10° and therefore they need to be much longer than they think. This was about 12 inches and the angle must have been 30° or greater. We found an extra piece of wood to raise it slightly and I made a run at it cursing under my breath. I heard the crack of the absolutely inadequate piece of wood but was relieved when I landed safely in the lobby. The slightly shamefaced husband was sent off to find a longer piece of wood. The corridor was unexpectedly narrow and it took all my navigational skills to avoid gouging great channels out of the walls. Once inside our room, it was large and airy with a patio door onto a little balcony that overlooked an ornamental pond complete with live ducks. It was quite delightful. The ensuite toilet was large with a a sizeable shower, but heedless architects or builders were in evidence once again. It was necessary to step up into it which there was absolutely no way I could do without assistance. It's extraordinary the number of bathrooms I've come across since being disabled, which are described as fully accessible but are far from it. Disability doesn't seem to include people with very little or no upper body strength who are unable to use handgrips and rails to pull up on. Another ubiquitous difficulty I've discovered, even in wet rooms, is the ludicrous provision of a little seat that pulls down from the wall, presumably for some kind of security. However, the angle at which one has to sit up is 90°, which is impossible for anyone like me. Furthermore, the shower controls are often beyond one's reach or require the flexibility of torso of a Paralympic athlete. These not inconsiderable problems aside, it was a charming B&B which provided a deliciously full English breakfast enabling us to explore the hidden crannies of East Anglia.

Cathedrals exude power, beauty, human ingenuity and virility. Perhaps that's why I have such a passion for mediaeval architecture when I'm not at all religious. In fact, I'm strongly anti religious, but I distinguish sharply between the practice and the product. I believe religious buildings of all types are an important part of our culture and their appreciation should not be restricted to the pious and the privileged. Today, most of them ask for a voluntary donation from visitors sometimes bordering on intimidation. This is what we found at Norwich. A dubious welcome by church officials was followed by a peremptory gesture towards the contribution box. Being a bloody-minded individual, I went over and studiously regarded it but kept my hand in my pocket. I would rather they charged a specific fee, or received a donation from the State, or both, to maintain them. After this trying ritual, we found that people in wheelchairs were admitted for free! I must, therefore, congratulate all cathedrals that I have visited in this country for providing excellent access for wheelchair users. The only criticism I would make of Norwich in this respect, is that I could not open some of the doors from a wheelchair, or get into the toilets, without assistance. A brand-new visitor centre, with excellent facilities and a refectory with a superb wheelchair lift system, was unaccountably inaccessible for the independent wheelchair user. It is astonishing how architects take on board some of these requirements but fail to go the whole hog.

At Norwich, the rain relentlessly battered us whenever we stepped outside. There was no respite until the early afternoon. The National Trust Handbook was our permanent companion from which we discovered there was a place worthy of our attention on the route back north to our accommodation. It was a late mediaeval country mansion and estate that had been owned by the Boleyn family. Given its size and opulence it must have been a royal reward from Henry VIII to his bride's family, the Boleyns. Like most National Trust properties, I expected to gain access to the ground floors but not elsewhere. I was delightfully surprised to discover a previous owner had skilfully installed an elevator down a service corridor and hidden by oak panelling. It allowed me access to what was probably the best room in the house. This was a typical Elizabethan parlour, which had been elongated into a gallery delivering a profusion of natural light. A row of elegant narrow windows illuminated the magnificent displays of huge family portraits and local landscapes. One half of this airy space was given over to a music salon and on the day of our visit, a single professional musician was playing a lute. It was magically entrancing listening to the historically evocative sound in its authentic surroundings. It also enabled one to admire the exquisitely delicate, rich and ornate plaster cornices with the imposing central ceiling decorations in the shape of a bull, the family's motif. For me, this was the highlight of the visit and of the whole weekend. I can understand the National Trust's policy of not providing lifts for visitors to access the upper stories of the properties in their care because it would seriously detract from the historical character of the buildings. They are aware, nevertheless, how this discriminates against wheelchair users and therefore provide videos on interactive TVs to accommodate them.

Peterborough and Ely cathedrals were next in line for our scrutiny. Ely is one of the most impressive I have ever seen.The setting is unique. In the distance projects its dominating profile. It's as if one is transported back into the Middle Ages, before towns and traffic erupted to scar the landscape, and these great houses of God proclaimed his power and glory all around. The exceptional central tower showers light into every corner, where there is no hiding from the all-seeing presence. There is an innocent Palladian atmosphere surrounding this time-locked edifice. Fleecy fields, time honoured Oaks and a tiny trilling stream provide a vision of what it was like when it was first hewn out of the earth. Ely is a place not to avoid, whatever one's beliefs, - a spiritual vortex to enhance well-being whatever one's state of mind or body. I felt I could have lingered there forever. Inside, the custodians demonstrate their contact with contemporary life by the fascinating displays depicting a historical narrative of the surrounding lands to the present, as well as their missionary work around the world and among the homeless in the UK.

Majorca

Winter had come for Carol and I with a vengeance in the New Year of 2015, with a threat of no release. It was necessary to take this by the throat and demand the return of the sun and warmth to our exhausted bodies. One particularly bleak day, we stormed off to the travel agents after having become weary of searching the Internet for something to meet our needs. Our hopes were fragile but the results were brilliant. Having identified Majorca as a suitable destination, they did everything else, ensuring that all transport and accommodation were accessible for me. Special travel insurance had to be arranged because MND was uninsurable with our annual package. We rang the MND Association and found they could provide us with a list of insurers who would quote for people with the condition. There were six on the list but two wanted so much information that it was not worth pursuing. Others, however, would quote with a letter from the medical team to confirm that I was fit and able to fly. We had an appointment at the breathing unit coming up soon, so we were able to combine that with a flight test, costing £50. I was given the okay and the actual premium we had to pay was only £60, though some insurers had quoted double that. It pays to shop around!

We had selected a resort well away from the raucous nightlife attracting the 20 and 30 year old some things in the full foetid flush of their youth. These were resorts close to Palma, the capital city, but we chose a quieter location on the north-east coast of a large crescent-shaped sandy bay. It turned out to be ideal because of a long seafront promenade that provided me with ample scope to drive up and down it on a hired mobility scooter.

An unforeseen, and what might have become a very challenging part of our holiday, was right at the beginning of our journey. At Palma airport there was no one to assist us, unlike our departure from Birmingham. It was like a scene from a Charlie Chaplin film: Carol was pushing me along in the wheelchair with one hand, pulling luggage behind her with the other and I was straining to push/pull another without much success. Had it not been for two fellow passengers on the aeroplane, whom we had befriended, we would have been stranded. Another obstacle was baggage recovery. In addition to the portable hand luggage, we added a monstrous black bag with no other place for it to go but across my legs. Although the holiday claimed to be disabled accessible, that was straining veracity. If I'd not been able to scramble on board the coach, I would have been carried on board like a sack of potatoes. When we arrived at the hotel, everything else fell into its expected place. The hired estate car was waiting for us as arranged. At Reception, my eyes lit up when I saw a row of gleaming mobility scooters on charge and for hire. Like a child in a sweet shop, I had to have one. Despite the fact the cost of the mobility scooter exceeded that of the estate car, I knew it was going to be a necessity.

16° C seemed like the ambient inside temperature of a fridge but it was still appreciably warmer then being in the UK. There were also other unforeseen irritants like our room being on the fourth floor. Each time we sallied forth, we had to play bingo waiting for the lift. The prize was the arrival of a tiny box which was so small it required the dismantling of my foot plates in order to get inside. Nevertheless, the room was acceptably spacious containing two single beds and an ensuite. Mornings were precarious. Like a chimpanzee I had to swing from the top of the flimsy shower curtain to the shower head. There were absolutely no handrails! Again, I found salvation in my upper body remaining stronger than my lower. The loo was built for Humpty Dumpty and my feet dangled 4 inches from the floor. It was obviously a disabled toilet built for the tallest people in Europe, the Dutch.

Our first entry into the restaurant shocked us. We were by far the youngest there. In the midst of a chomping, gregarious horde of octogenarians, like locusts having swept in from the north, there was a mountain of food to feed the army of Genghis Khan for six months. The locusts encircled the seductive buffets of European, Majorcan and Spanish delicacies until there was hardly a scrap remaining. Each night provided something new and enticing to the palate. Because I couldn't carry a tray, Carol wheeled me around these delectable culinary offerings, which I then had to choose and commit to memory so that having returned me to my table, she could scramble to fill both our dishes whilst something still remained.

In the evening, entertainment was available on the ground floor, the centre of which was a large cocktail bar. Here Carol delighted in ordering the speciality of the house, *Sex on the Beach*. Stoically the waiters kept a straight face whenever this salaciously-named drink was ordered but it was guaranteed to break the ice in a new crowd of acquaintances. The singalongs, bingo and the general entertainment weren't particularly to our taste, so we sauntered a little way along the promenade to follow the setting sun.

That week the promenade was barely alive, as the season was just getting underway. There were copious empty spaces for my scooter and Carol on a hire bike to race each other along the strand. We stopped at will for coffee and lunch, but our preferred venues were those catering for the German tourist. Invariably we found the catering and choice of food superior to those responding to English tastes. We could believe we were having two holidays for one with German and Spanish beer available on tap. It was a good time that I can look back upon now with fond memories. I was still able to raise a glass of beer to my lips and use a knife and fork in a stumbling fashion. Happily, I was able to toilet myself and thrust from my mind what would happen in the future.

Most people at the hotel hadn't bothered to hire a rental car but I'm glad we did. For us, a holiday is the delight in stripping away the tourist façade. There was the visit to a little market town nearby with actual locals that lived real lives. Twice a week, it became a leather goods market. Most of the stallholders were African retailers and it was really too much to expect to find a bargain amongst their 'leather 'goods. But, one of Carol's greatest passions is to hunt through stalls piled high with bags and scarves looking for the holy Grail - a 'bargain '. I liked to practise my Spanish, although it wasn't really necessary as the Africans spoke English well. Meanwhile, they would talk volubly about the merits of their goods and smell a determined 'bargain-hunter ' from 50 m away. She had her eye on a little blue bag for which they wanted €40, claiming it was real leather. She haggled them down to €20 but didn't agree a sale because there were other stalls that needed to be ransacked. When it began to drizzle lazily, we escaped to an authentically attractive café/restaurant for a coffee. There was no one in when we arrived and we were served immediately by a pretty young woman in her mid 20s. I worked my Spanish magic which produced a deliciously strong espresso and a little almond cake. I was feeling quite pleased with myself for having accomplished this little trick until another tourist entered to whom she spoke in perfect English. She was English and had lived there with her parents since she was a young child. Naturally, she had an encyclopaedic knowledge of the area and was able to recommend places we wouldn't have thought of visiting. Carol then decided she must go back to the stall where she had seen her 'bargain 'whilst I remained in the restaurant to save the rigmarole of getting back into the wheelchair, ordering another coffee. The first coffee I'd drunk was a pretty explosive double espresso and now, suffering from the narcotic effects of that, I dangerously ordered another. When Carol proudly returned with her prize, we returned to the car in order to take a little sightseeing tour. However, as soon as I was sat in the passenger seat I began to experience severe palpitations accompanied by severe sweating and clamminess. 'This is it, 'I thought, ' I'm having a heart attack. I'm going to die in this foreign country and I haven't even finished the holiday! ' Like a hammer blow, it struck both of us at the same time - I'd drunk the equivalent of four single espressos, one after the other like an alcoholic after a year's abstinence. It was a very high price to pay for such excellent coffee but one that I wouldn't pay again. It took a couple of hours and two paracetamol before I returned to normal. I didn't drink another cup of coffee for the rest of that holiday.

Palma Cathedral was an unavoidable sight to see, for us. So, on a disappointingly drizzly day we navigated our way from Cala Bona to the capital of the island. We knew exactly where to go, thanks to our European sat nav. Negotiating the only multilane motorway in the whole of Majorca, a combination of instinct and modern technology allowed us to navigate directly to the subterranean car park adjacent to the Cathedral. Outside, we emerged into a great mediaeval Plaza from which the ramparts of the city rose impossibly up presenting us with no obvious entrance. We could see the Cathedral clearly rising up from beyond the ramparts, steps everywhere blocking our way. As our eyes adjusted, we spied an entrance into this complex of mediaeval defences arriving at a steep ramp up which it appeared our way led. I took one look at it, with its 45° angle and steep slope and told Carol that not even with the hounds of hell behind me would I be induced to go up it. Then intricate little alleyways began to materialise to reveal a secret route zigzagging up towards the area of the Cathedral. Unfortunately, this was all cobbled! Poor Carol bravely pushed me all the way up those unforgiving mediaeval streets until we arrived at an obscure and eminently missable entrance around the back, the front door being sealed off. Here there was a small kiosk to take the entry fee and we could see a ramp to avoid steps into the Cathedral itself. The only problem was a six-inch high step to get onto its level. If I hadn't been able to stand up out of my wheelchair onto it, it would have been impossible to enter. Paradoxically, once inside there were ramps everywhere. It just didn't make sense. We didn't have to pay either because of my disability, so it wasn't as if the Cathedral authorities were trying to deter disabled visitors. When we queried it, we were told it was because of some regulation to do with access from or to the street, a bylaw of local government, not the Cathedral. There was a bizarre, almost Caribbean like feeling about the inside. Its greatest glory was a huge circular stained-glass window facing West that must have poured in a kaleidoscope of light when the sun was permitted to emerge from the late winter sky. It was enchantingly arresting but we did not experience much of it because poor weather intervened and the temperature within the Cathedral was much lower than outside. It was a veritable fridge, so we saw what we could, admiring the relics, religious icons and the tapestries and then escaped into a marginally warmer drizzling rain. It was difficult negotiating the cobbles so we gave up the attempt to explore the main town beyond and dejectedly took shelter in a dreary little café nearby where we had some kind of hot pasty to warm us up. That's all we saw of Palma.

Various excursions were laid on, but we had our own transport and preferred to travel around independently. However, there was one excursion that took our fancy to a cabaret somewhere in the north-west of the island promising an excellent meal, good wine and first-rate entertainment. As a number of other people were going from the hotel whom we knew and it was a couple of days before the end of the holiday, we decided to purchase tickets. These weren't cheap at €130 each but we thought it would probably be worth it. And it certainly was. Everything was superb, especially the entertainment with the high rise trapeze artists, top-notch singers and dancers. It was the kind of entertainment that we were not used to and revelled in its novelty. There were absolutely no problems with access. At one point, a sort of interval, people got up from the tables and began to dance. Carol was visiting the loo at this point and missed a remarkable happening. I was dancing - in my chair! I was so absorbed with it, the music and the atmosphere, I engaged in what can only be described as chair dancing. I still had some upper body strength and core flexibility, but when Carol returned I was exhausted and the following day, found it difficult to get out of bed. We both agreed it had been one of the high points of our holiday.

We had booked that holiday at the last minute in the full knowledge that if I suddenly deteriorated we would not be able to go and we would lose the total cost of the booking. It vindicated our approach but I wished we had taken more risks in that respect and gone on more such ventures. As it was, it raised our confidence and encouraged us to plan more adventurously. It confirmed in striking terms that my rate of deterioration was slower than we had been led to believe from the prognosis.

Devon

My lovely daughter, Ashley, had decided she was going to do something for dad. She is a fearless Cumbrian firefighter benefiting from the National Fire Services' recuperation establishment in Devon. Lying 15 miles south-west of Exeter, it is a perfect spot for exploring that lovely county and coastline. It consists of an elegant Georgian house surrounded by 300 acres. On site, congenial well-sized chalets provide extra accommodation and give access to gorgeous woodland walks and fisheries. It is available for service members and their families to book for holidays and recuperation. In April 2015, almost 5 months after diagnosis, I could still manage with care to walk 20 paces in a stumbling fashion. Remarkably, I drove for the first hour until my arms became dangerously weak, when Carol and Ashley took over. A recently purchased WAV (wheelchair accessible vehicle) proved to be a fantastic workhorse. My wonderful power-wheelchair was loaded up in the back and packed all round with luggage and other essential equipment I required. It transformed the holiday as a result of its amazing versatility. A comfortable range of 7 to 10 miles, depending upon terrain, allowed us to tackle otherwise impossible destinations. Even the precipitous streets of Totnes were well within its scope as was a seascape nature trail from Exeter to Exmouth, along the Exe estuary. This was a scary route at the beginning, when I had to negotiate a metre wide path atop the sea wall without any safety rails. It didn't help that I was also still getting used to the controls. In Exmouth the battery was virtually flat, but the little steam train that plies that route was available to return us safely to our starting point.

One of the most memorable trips we took that holiday was when Ashley and I took the river cruiser from Totnes to Dartmouth. With some difficulty, I made it down the landing steps onto the boat with a little help where we found a seat inside protecting us from the cutting wind and sporadic bouts of rain. Carol was to rendezvous with us in Dartmouth with the life-saving power chair. To me, the unknown River Dart was an aesthetic revelation. The river is alive with every sort of creature indigenous to its shores. It must be a divine haven for the bird twitchers and fly-fishers that we could see indulging their art as the river pursued its wilful way to the sea.

Impressive country piles like Agatha Christie's Greenway and Coleton Fishacre give testimony to the exclusivity enjoyed at various times by the very wealthy on the Dart estuary. Dartmouth itself is a fitting little fishing port that complements the grandeur of the river. Often infested with tourists, it is almost impossible to find a parking space. Carol was confronted with this problem when she arrived, but there were free spaces for disabled vehicles, which she made use of quite legitimately. However, she roused general consternation when she was seen to jump out of the driver's seat, run around to the rear and reverse my power chair down the ramp. They didn't know of course that she was bringing it for me at the landing jetty where our cruise boat docked. With increasing nervousness, I saw her wobbling unsteadily from side to side along a narrow pavement. She had not yet fully mastered the beast and I could feel the panic welling up in me when she then turned onto the even narrower gantry leading to the boat. I was certain she would end up in the water. These fears proved to be baseless and with relief I saw her come to an almost graceless stop when I took her place.

It was a perfect holiday in many ways, not the least because we made it work. But, it was also a sad reminder of the time when, three years before, Carol and I had driven to Totnes with our bikes and taken off on a day's hard ride into the hills. But one shouldn't dwell too long on the past for fear of relapsing into painful despair - much   better is to look forward. The prize is more lovely memories, as it should be.

Cornwall in June

Devon had boosted my confidence and I was eager to set out again, this time down memory lane. As a child, I had lived for two glorious years just outside Falmouth and I wanted to see it one more time. 15 years ago Carol and I had taken a touring holiday with Alex, our young son, but this was to be different. I was anxious to rekindle the memories of my seven year old self. How different would it be? Would there be anything left of that lost world?

We identified a sizeable farmhouse cottage, a few miles from Falmouth, spacious enough for Carol's son, Terry, and his family including Alex. It was the perfect location for whatever direction we decided to explore. We had no choice really because an exhaustive search for accessible accommodation in Falmouth drew a blank. Despite the fickle English weather, so typical of June, the microclimate around Falmouth delivered reasonably acceptable temperatures. There was my old primary school, now an art college, where I learned the recorder and to fear the wrath of the traditional headmaster who didn't flinch from laying about him with his whistling came. As if it were yesterday, the memories flooded into my synapses, a bewildering variety of the good and the bad. The narrow, harbour side High Street of Falmouth hadn't changed and I was overjoyed at rediscovering the magical ship's chandler's shop that had so hypnotised me with its Aladdin's cave treasures. There also was the tree-lined town square to which as children we had flocked on Saturday mornings not to miss the Lone Ranger, Lassie the Wonder Dog or Popeye the

Sailor. Wealth and modernity have arrived in Falmouth but not to the extent that it has ruined its old-world atmosphere.

Palm trees and sand strewn roads add a tropical feel to the approach to Gillingvase beach where, as a child, I had spent a postcolonial holiday with nostalgic parents, not long returned from and still pining for a very Empire-conscious New Zealand. The little pre-war hotel was on the edge of the beach fronted by a long tropical garden with frondeed plants in profusion. We simply dashed out barefoot from the main entrance directly through the garden to plunge into the gentle surf.

Prior to our departure for Cornwall, I had purchased a new Sterling Diamond mobility scooter. It has a maximum speed of 8 miles per hour and is equipped for travelling on the highway with large wheels enabling it to traverse rough ground. It also has a formidable range of 25 miles that is more than enough for what I needed. Periodically I would take off on my own for a few miles' jaunt down the lanes or through the town revelling in the independence. Then, I still had sufficient upper arm strength to steer it safely. Regrettably, those days have dwindled into the past.

The quintessential beauty of Falmouth can only be fully experienced from the water. Its harbour-side captures the timeless essence of people living by the sea. By far the best way of entering this magical world is to take the ferry trip from Falmouth to Truro for which one must embark from one of the precarious jetties which, other than at high tide, require one to negotiate the slippery, seaweed steps onto the boat. The manual wheelchair was hauled aboard as if it were made of cork by a very replica of Popeye the sailor. Entering the bobbing ferry required fearless dependence on strong hands but eventually I found myself comfortably positioned in the stern with magnificent views all around. The Carrick roads, where the Fal and Truro rivers meet before they issue forth into the open sea, are a magnet for shipping of all kinds. It was thrilling to be in the middle of all this with the sun twinkling from the waves and graceful sloops coursing by. The tide was out as we approached Truro but our questions multiplied as we realised we were nowhere in sight of the city and the waterway was too shallow for the boat. To our consternation, we discovered at low tide the river isn't navigable so passengers have to disembark and climb aboard a double-decker bus to complete the journey. We could see the bus stop was up a slight hill, three quarters of a mile away. However, we hadn't reckoned on the doughty Cornish sailors who came to our assistance and pushed me all the way. They also insisted they would be there when we returned if it was by bus. And they were! It was a memorable adventure, added to by being able to visit the Cathedral, thus bagging another Gothic trophy.

A Daring Plan

Success in Cornwall inspired us to take on a more audacious project. The proposal was to hire an apartment in Languedoc, southern France, inviting family and friends to share it with us over a two-week period. We had acquaintances who managed a number of private holiday apartments in Canaules, 30 miles from Nimes. September was the chosen month when temperatures would be around the mid-20s centigrade. The challenge was travelling there with the equipment I needed. Air travel was out of the question because of this. So how were we going to do it? Firstly, we knew we could get down there very fast by high speed train, the TGV, which departed from St Pancras at 8 AM and arrived in Avignon at 3 PM the same day. Wonderful, especially as I had never travelled on this train before and hurtling through the French countryside at 200 miles an hour was particularly appealing. Disability status also allowed one to get first class seats at half the price. The other part of this cunning plan was that my son, Alex, would drive our van from home to rendezvous with us at the TGV station in Avignon. This required detailed planning which was accomplished perfectly with Alex arriving only 15 minutes after we disembarked at Avignon. It was a terrific way to travel with stewards pampering as with airline service. There were only three stops on the whole journey: at Ashford in Kent, then Lille and Lyons. Such a journey would have been unthinkable 50 years ago -from the Midlands to the south of France without flying in less than a day. The only disturbing part of the entire journey was a picture of modern Britain, homeless people in sleeping bags at 6:30 AM hunkered down for the night between the beautiful brick recesses of St Pancras. From Avignon to our destination was an hour by car and when we arrived our friends, John and Judy, had prepared a sumptuous buffet of French cheeses, cold meats, salad and wine.

The apartments were set in the centre of a tiny village, an island in the middle of profusely expansive vineyards. Bicycles were available for all and my mobility scooter set the pace in exploring the many small towns, markets, historical sites and roadside wine tastings throughout the area. My scooter became a curious spectacle for the locals who referred to it as la petite voiture. In fact, I only saw one other mobility scooter in the whole time that we were there, which turned out to be owned by another English person. Unlike Britain, where one comes across disability scooters, mobility aids of all kinds and where it is unusual not to see a disabled person out and about in town centres, there was a complete lack of them in France. This is a mystery because the facilities in restaurants for disabled toilets and disabled parking are as plentiful as in the UK. Is there a negative status which is so strong in the country that it deters people with disabilities from getting around outside or simply a lack of equipment? I would be surprised if there was because I found nothing but genuine help and support from locals and all the places I visited. On one occasion, having repaired to a neighbouring village where there was a reputedly good restaurant, the most ferocious rainfall suddenly occurred and we were sent scurrying for shelter. Inside the restaurant, knowledgeable locals were happily soaking up the warmth from the pizza oven which was working overtime. The only way for me to gain entry into this gastronomic Shangri-La was via a pair of French doors opening onto the main street. As there had already been one or two heavy downpours in the previous few days, a plank had been nailed across the base of these doors to prevent flooding. But the owner of the restaurant didn't bat an eyelid when he realised what needed to be done. Without asking, he took a hammer and knocked away the plank and I bounced into the restaurant almost sending the whole company flying as if they were skittles in a bowling alley. This happy jovial crowd gladly made way for me to get to my table where I joined my friends and family to enjoy two hours of feasting and drinking.

This holiday was all the more appreciated because I could indulge myself in the French language and culture, which I didn't think I'd ever be able to again. Names of places I knew from maps and history such as Montpelier, Avignon and the Pont du Garde revealed themselves in person. My only regret was that I couldn't do what Robert Louis Stevenson had done nearly 200 years before i.e. travel through the foothills of the Cevennes on a donkey. What a magnificent area! It also stimulated my interest in the mysterious Cathars and how they were mercilessly persecuted for over a hundred years in the 13th century by the Roman Catholic Church and the King of France.

There was a swimming pool outside the apartments for use by the residents and I looked at it enviously as those around me cooled off in the late afternoon heat. With temperatures nearing 30° C in the second week of the holiday, it became a favoured haunt. I knew I needed a hoist otherwise there would be trouble but egged on by Carol I was convinced I too could immerse myself in this gloriously cool pool. There were steps, after all, in one corner. I was encouraged to put on a pair of water wings to keep me buoyant, not being strong enough in the arms, and launched myself into the water. My three year old grandson, Oscar, was thrilled by the spectacle and I became the target of much water slapping. After a few hesitant attempts, I found I could sort of float on my back, a curiously liberating experience. What I hadn't really thought about was how to get out of the swimming pool because I had no strength in my legs, even in water, to step up nor any arm strength to be able to pull myself out. With some help I managed to sit on one of the submerged steps and then Andy, my daughter Ashley's partner, who is built like a bodybuilder, physically hauled me out. In the process, however, he almost dislocated one of my arms so that was my one and only immersion in the pool. It had been good, but now it was time to return to the more serious business of drinking good wine and sampling the delicious local produce.

The apartment wasn't really designed for someone as disabled as I was but they did a very good job in trying to make me comfortable and accommodate my needs. I scored a few marks on the walls, but they didn't complain. They had provided ramps so I could access the apartment by wheelchair or scooter easily from outside. The shower was a different problem but with the aid of a plastic garden chair and Carol, I managed to remain hygienic for the week. More disconcertingly, especially when I was sat on the loo, was my personal discovery that there are scorpions in southern France!. Yes, they have scorpions, which can give you a nasty sting. I've since learned there are in fact small scorpions in the south of England too. Carol found one in our bedroom that was 3 inches long, but it didn't last long! The essential advice: shake out your trousers, underwear and socks before you put them on.

The return journey was similar to the outward one, except we had still yet to make arrangements to get to Avignon for the train as Alex would have to leave before us. We had decided it was better to rendezvous with him in Ashford than to stay in London overnight or continue travelling through the night. Once again, all went very much to plan except for something beyond our control. Courtesy of UK border control, the whole train had to disembark on the return journey at Lille, complete with baggage, to go through UK customs. This took a good hour and wasn't something we had to do on the outward journey. Of course, disabled passengers were prioritised and I was surprised to see about 30 more people in scooters or wheelchairs disgorged from the 30 car train at this point.

It had been a daunting prospect, but we had succeeded. The moral of the story must be to avoid imposing unambitious aims on oneself. We knew when we were booking everything that I might not be well enough to travel and that there would be no recompense from any travel insurance if that were the case. We were right to take the risk and I would recommend anyone else in the same circumstances to do the same.

Chapter 3

Second Stage of My MND Journey

So good, so far but how long would this last? My standing strength was beginning to wane imperceptibly. The day I fell sprawling down the metal ramps outside my room, was when I was forced to admit that I had reached a new stage in my deterioration. Fortunately, my mobility scooter had saved me. Otherwise I would have continued to roll off the patio and into the garden, a not inconsiderable drop. It reminded me of a similar incident the year before, when I was still working part-time and awaiting a diagnosis. I had parked my car and walked up numerous steps towards the main college entrance, but as I was coming up the last few steps I fell inexplicably. I had fallen full length with my bag and books flying in all directions. It was as if I had tripped over something but there was nothing there. With hindsight I realised that it must have been a consequence of drop foot, which is a condition of MND. It wasn't particularly pronounced in me, but my left foot and leg were not functioning as they should. The physiotherapist prescribed a walking frame. At the beginning, I scorned its use until I came to depend on it totally even for just a few steps to get to the wet room.

By late summer 2015, I was struggling to go up and down stairs to the bedroom. Carol had to heave me up whilst coming down I slid on my backside with the risk of hurtling down headfirst. The cottage dates back to 1640 and it just isn't practical to fit a chairlift. Nor would that have been feasible for long as I was rapidly losing upper body strength.

Carol and the Occupational Therapist were urging me to move permanently downstairs. This was a devastating psychological blow. It reminded me of my old maternal grandparents living in the front room of my aunt's house before they died. Carol was much more practical - I think it's how she deals with the whole emotional mess. She had already planned everything and decided the solution was to knock down an inner wall allowing for a double bed so we could try to carry on as usual. When they raised it with me, I was vehemently opposed. I just didn't want to accept that I had become an invalid and like some aged, dependent relative would be consigned to a room on the ground floor. However, the logic was irrefutable and I knew I would have to concede. The downstairs ensuite bathroom was easily converted into a wet room. This is one of the worst things about the illness. There is no hope of improvement or even remission and one therefore must plan for the next stage of disability. If not, life becomes impossible. Out went the bath, in came a shower which I now rely on absolutely. I chose my own bathroom suite, in an attractive, grey marble tiling, reflecting my masculine tastes. It took nearly 3 weeks for building works to be completed during which time I was evacuated to the main lounge from which I was able also to access a commode in a small recess under the stairs. The dust was everywhere but I wasn't lonely and the builders proved to be both considerate and humorous companions. By November, it was finished. I would no longer have to risk life and limb sliding precariously downstairs. We were therefore able to delay the time when we would no longer be able to share a bed and I had to use a hospital bed.

For a long time, I could still happily access the dining room table, even though it was in my manual wheelchair, and enjoy socialising with friends and family adding to my quality-of-life.

I have always been a sociable person, though I am not afraid to spend time on my own. I enjoy extending my knowledge of languages, reading widely and writing. I have also found support and comfort from neighbours who would periodically drop-in for a chat and a coffee, and whom I would also visit until it became impossible for me to access their houses. Most of my friends' houses became inaccessible after the first year and 1/2 after diagnosis, but those who were really my friends didn't allow that to be a bar to our continued friendship. I still have friends who continue to see me on a regular basis, sometimes preparing food and bringing wine to take the burden off Carol. It is also possible for me to dine out at some of the local pubs and restaurants, having first reconnoitred them for ease of access. It's always a pleasure to be able to do this with friends or just the two of us.

I have been hurt, however, by some ex-colleagues, whom I considered friends, who have distanced themselves from me, even to the extent of walking the other way if they see me coming in town so they won't have to engage me in conversation. Others, who affect a hospitable greeting and friendly overtures at certain gatherings, where they have been surprised by my presence, simply have not been in touch at all. Neither by email, mobile or letter. Can one blame them? I don't know. I can appreciate that for some people it is just too hurtful or embarrassing or they feel socially gauche. But, I would say to them, I would appreciate it. When I have had old friends, ex-students and even unknown members of the general public contact me or engage me in discussion, it has been an uplifting experience. Is it perhaps an inability to deal with one's own mortality that prevents them from contacting me? Or is it, an inability to know how to talk to someone who is terminally ill? If so, it is time they faced these existential realities and reject the current taboo surrounding death and dying. Another response that I have had to deal with has come from either a close friend or even a relative, that I find particularly distasteful and even ghoulish. It begins by them asking how I am to which I usually reply, 'I'm fine, thanks '. However, this doesn't seem to satisfy them. They want to dig deeper into my emotional bank and ask, 'yes, but how are you really? ', accompanied by a look of grave concern. I don't know what they expect me to do but I am not prepared to disclose my innermost feelings to them at the drop of a hat. It's almost as if they want me suddenly to breakdown emotionally and confess all. I usually end up being quite rude to them.

At first, when one begins to use a wheelchair one feels extremely self-conscious, a little hypersensitive. I remember one particular occasion early after my diagnosis, when Carol and I visited Ironbridge, one New Year's Day. Morris dancers were performing, a sight we had seen many times before, and we went over to join the festive crowd gathered on the bridge. In the midst of this densely packed audience, I felt quite small and vulnerable, and without any warning began to weep. I'm not sure whether this was because of a particular tendency with MND for emotional expression, called lability, or a simple case of self-pity, seeing these jolly, sweating individuals of my own age enjoying themselves by cavorting in this way. Had I been standing, I don't think I would have had that reaction. The experience differs, I think, according to whether one is in a manual wheelchair, pushed by someone, or driving a power chair independently and in control. Another advantage with the power chair is its height which is not far off that of an average adult. Gradually confidence grows until it is difficult not to feel resentful of those who suddenly dart across one's path risking serious injury from a 135 kg machine with a top speed of 4 miles an hour. Fortunately, I have become extremely adept driving it and even unwittingly jousting with cathedrals. Nevertheless, I have had to pay a number of visits to Wheelchair Services to have repairs made and parts replaced. The service in Shropshire is excellent and completely free. Although it is a private company now, its funding comes from the NHS. Three cheers for the NHS.

December 2015 was going to be my second Christmas after diagnosis. I was still able to invite friends around and share in the festivities with them. This time, however, I think I underestimated what I could do. Let's be honest, more specifically, how much I could drink. Some of my friends, nay all my friends, enjoy a drink or two. Good quality wine flowed freely, G&T's, excellent malt whiskeys and rich ports were coiffed with abandon. It was hardly surprising therefore, and for this I cannot blame my friends, that I suffered a severe attack of gout, which I have been prone to for the past 15 years. Normally, when a flareup occurs I take some pills and it subsides in a day or two, but this time it didn't. No one to blame but myself of course! Whether it was a curse or a blessing I can't decide. Initially, there was no question about it because I was in agony, especially when I had to use the walking frame to go to the loo. The usual tablets wouldn't clear it, so I had to ring the doctor for something else. He prescribed a course of steroids. In three days I went from being suicidal to euphoria and at the heart of the festivities, organising a carol singing and play reading. My mind was racing and half the night I spent composing the play whilst in the morning I was still holding forth at a terrific rate of knots. This went on for over two weeks when I was in such a jolly mood that Carol wanted me to remain on steroids forever. In fact, we asked the GP if this was possible but he said he didn't know enough about MND and would have to write to the specialist neurologist to find out. The neurologist's response was a decisive negative, it wasn't normal to use this kind of medication for such a purpose. Pity! I then had to be weaned off the steroids over a further two week period experiencing withdrawal symptoms of severe headaches. Since then, I have been extremely careful not to overindulge and take care not to eat too many of my

54

favourite foods which are high in prurines such as spinach, wholemeal brown bread, oily fish, crustaceans and beer. Fortunately, there are still other good foods around which I can enjoy. As for beer, I can only ever drink a maximum of two halves at one session. The days of my youth when I could consume 5 to 6 pints are long since over. Fortuitously, wine and whiskey are not so problematic for gout sufferers, although it does depend on the volume of each consumed, especially together!

In the New Year, the plan was for Carol to return to work for two days. She had taken sick leave for over a year now since I was diagnosed and her employers had been extremely sympathetic to our plight. This was when we crossed another psychological line when it was decided that I would have to accept a carer for those days when Carol was working. She had been having to get me out of bed, washed and dressed along with a sandwich and drink for lunch before she left the house at 8:15 AM. This had become all too difficult for both of us, and, though I could still see to my own personal care, there was always a risk of me falling when I tried to go to the loo or get lunch from the kitchen. We had bought a special telephone, which I could answer if it rang without getting up to pick up the receiver, sensitive enough to pick up cries for help from the wet room, but this was still not enough.

 I was still getting weaker and weaker and it was increasingly dangerous for me to toilet myself so we arranged for a personal carer for two days a week. This was Graham and he turned out to be an absolute gem of a man. He was only three years younger than I was, having taken early retirement from the prison service but he was not ready to give up work. Graham proved to be a cut above the average carer because of his meticulousness, his intelligence and his commitment to duty of care. It is not easy accepting personal care but eventually I had to and he made it easier because of who he was and the fact that we had an excellent rapport. It was about late winter 2016 when Graham first entered our lives. At the beginning, his hours were limited to about an hour a day, extending to 1 hour and 1/2 when I needed the personal care. At this stage, after Graham had gone and for those two days Carol was working, I was often on my own except for a friend, John, who would come and encourage me to come out for a pub lunch. This was great but there were still times when I began to experience long hours on my own. I don't really mind this solitude so long as I am sharply focused on something, whether it is reading, writing or listening to music. However, this time it was different. I think it was the anticlimax of coming off the steroids in the dreariness of the New Year that combined to channel my thinking to end-of-life matters. I poured over the MNDA research blogs looking for a breakthrough. There were indications of some exciting research, but I knew it would be years before it came to fruition. I began therefore to consider what I would do as I deteriorated, which I was doing, month by month and it was not something I could ignore. At one stage, my thoughts became extremely bleak as the next entry, which I wrote at the time, conveys.

Darkness

I drew close to the edge of darkness today, hovering on the brim, attracted by the infinite blackness, knowing that if I went in there would be no return. What is this darkness? I know it is not Conrad's Darkness[3], when the veneer of civilisation is peeled away to reveal the primitive urges lying just below the surface of our existence. Or is there a trace of it, in the lure of the infinite, the unknowing in the face of the existential wonder of being that emerges when we face the prospect of ceasing to be? There is an attraction in losing oneself wholly in the universal. That cannot be dark! It sounds more like the Buddhist concept of enlightenment, when the individual, after years of training, achieves the ability to abnegate the self totally. Or, is it closer to Raskolnikov's torment in Dostoevsky's 'Crime and Punishment'[4], when, having defied the gods through his anarchic nihilism, he realises there is an absolute truth and a moral conscience that haunts him until he confesses all. He discovers that he is bound to his fellow man by bonds far stronger than his own intellect and learning. To deny those bonds will consign him to an individual hell that is the worst of all possible punishments, and he must seek atonement in confession becoming connected again to the world. Again, it is the theme of submersion of the individual, this time in the human collective. This is the humanist conclusion, whereas for Nietzsche[5] it is the point when humanity transcends its hitherto constricting mental constructs and evolves to a higher level replacing the gods. It is then that the individual becomes totally and profoundly alone. Is it at the point of death, that we become at once supermensch and nothing? When we see into the great infinite void of the universe confronted by the utter insignificance of our short and puny lives, as our consciousness dissolves into the infinity of nothingness, of not being?

What had brought me to this bleak, existential crossroad? Looking back, I now see the elements present to which both Dostoevsky and Nietzsche pointed. I was being left alone for two days a week as my wife struggled to carry on with her life having dropped from three days to two at work. Consequently, before we crossed the final Rubicon of arranging day care for me, I was sitting most of the time alone with my thoughts; a time I now recognise as one of the most dangerous. I would read and listen to music for a while but it was all too easy to slip into a period of introspective self-pity. It was now over a year since I had been diagnosed, and I had agreed reluctantly to move downstairs.

All the children were home for Christmas in 2015 and for a time we could pretend that I was not terminally ill. In the bleak twilight of the New Year, however, we had to accept the invasiveness and impersonality of having carers in our home. Yes, I thought, I am now officially an 'invalid' but worse than that was the reinforcement that I would continue to debilitate until I was dead. It was at this time that my thoughts repeatedly turned to my final days when I scoured the Internet for whatever information I could find, including sites like Exit, until I found Dignitas.

Chapter 4

Motor Neurone Disease and Other Neurological Conditions.

Motor Neurone Disease

Motor Neurone Disease[6] is a progressively insidious degenerative condition. It is a disease which kills the motor neurone receptors that transmit signals from the brain to the motor centres of the body i.e. the muscles. These signals cease to particular groups of muscles which atrophy becoming flabby and useless. It is not a disease of the muscles. There is no cure and only palliative care is available for relieving symptoms. It is a terminal illness, which means those with it continue to deteriorate until they die. It is also life shortening with the average life expectations varying according to what particular type of MND it is. There are at least four different types of the disease, although it is beginning to be thought now that there may be more varieties than previously envisioned. It is a rare condition primarily affecting people over the age of 50 years but it is not unknown in those who are considerably younger, even the early 20s and 30s. Its incidence is recorded as 2 to 3 per 100,000 of the population, which means that at any one time in the UK there are 5000 people living with it.

 As one of a series of neurological diseases, it is extremely difficult to diagnose and the time taken to do this, as it did in my case, may take 12 months or longer. There is no blood test to identify its presence, although research is working to do this. The tests that are carried out such as MRI, spinal taps, electrical blood tests are meant to eliminate other possible conditions. The final diagnosis will be made by a specialist MND neurologist who will make a clinical judgement from observations and enquiry after symptoms. He or she will be looking for the presence of fasciculations or muscle twitching, as well as looking for evidence of muscle wasting, particularly in the hands. The questions will concern sleeping pattern behaviour, gait and general fatigue. These, combined with the results of electrical tests, will facilitate a reasonably accurate diagnosis, although the particular type of MND may not be possible to spot at that time. Whichever type of MND is contracted, the process of neurodegenerative decay is the same. The electrical transmitters, known as neurones, are located both at the base of the skull and the spine and they are responsible for transferring a signal from the brain to receptors in the muscles which enable us to move. The source of the degeneration can be in either the upper neurones i.e base of the brain, or lower neurones i.e the base of the spine. The progression of the disease is frequently indicated by the location of its initial onset.

ALS (Amyotrophic lateral sclerosis) or Classic MND

Approximately 70% of people with MND will have ALS, known as Lou Gehrig's Disease in the USA. The average life expectation for someone with ALS is from 2 to 5 years, but it is very difficult for a neurologist to be more specific about the prognosis until symptoms signalling the onset of end-of-life occur. These range from loss of appetite, loss of weight, difficulty with breathing, loss of interest in issues and people around them, increasing tiredness and sleeping most of the day. According to my diagnosis, I have ALS which began in the lower neurones and therefore I was likely to lose control of my lower limbs early on, which I did. I was moreover, given 6 to 18 months to live based on my presenting symptoms, especially difficulties with breathing and not being able to sleep at night. The neurologist did, however, state this could only be a judgement based on current statistics. I could live longer or less than the parameters suggested. He was sufficiently concerned to arrange for me to be admitted to the Royal North Staffordshire hospital, which specialises in breathing conditions, as quickly as possible so I could be provided with NIV or Non-Invasive Ventilation. I was very happy about this because my nights had become a nightmare: every time I fell into a deep sleep or REM, I awoke because I stopped breathing. At his suggestion, I purchased a V shaped pillow so that I could sleep on my side for most of the night and obtain a modicum of a good night's rest. It certainly helped but when I finally got the NIV i.e. my Nippy 3+, I was given a whole new lease of life. I was very lucky in that I took to its use easily and I had no obstructions with secretions in my airways, which can occur with some types of MND. Whilst I was at the hospital, I was urged at the same time to have a P E G fitted, in the event that I developed problems with eating and swallowing, but I refused. Throughout my MND experience, to date this has not caused me any difficulties. For me also, it is a red line in the sand - when I am not able to eat and swallow properly, I do not wish to continue living. I made this very clear at the time to the doctors.

Progressive Bulbar Palsy

A particularly pernicious type of MND is Progressive Bulbar Palsy. This form of the disease originates in the upper neurones and very quickly inhibits the ability to swallow, move one's face and tongue. Eventually, 80% of sufferers will lose the ability to talk requiring the use of a small portable communicator. An immediate life-threatening feature of this variant of the disease is the inability to take food and fluids down the gullet. Unless one chooses to starve, a PEG (percutaneous endogenous gastrostomy) must be inserted into the stomach for sustenance. The average life expectation for this form of MND is less than ALS, from six months to 3 years.

PMA, PLS and Kennedys

Progressive Muscular Atrophy is a slower form of MND with a general life expectation of 10 years or more. It may leave the person unable to walk but with normal upper body strength. Another variant is Progressive Lateral Sclerosis and Kennedys which is very similar to MND because of the degeneration of motor neurones but is regarded as a separate and rare condition. These variants may be life shortening but they are not regarded usually as terminal. I sometimes wonder whether what I have is true classical ALS or one of these variants because it is well over three years since I was diagnosed and nearly 6 years from what I have identified in hindsight as early signs of onset. But I am always brought back to reality when I consider what I cannot do now being virtually paraplegic. On the other hand, although I rely heavily on NIV, I can still eat and drink and my voice remains strong.

Causes and treatment

It is still a mystery to researchers as to what causes MND. It is believed that certain genes, which have now been identified, are responsible for the genetic inheritance of the illness but having the gene does not automatically mean one contracts the disease. It is thought that approximately 5 to 10% of MND sufferers will have contracted it from a parental carrier and there is a test for this. In a small percentage of people, it may also affect the fronto-temporal lobe which means they will suffer from dementia. Speculative causes, that have not however been confirmed by research are: a highly active lifestyle, serious physical trauma, exposure to lead in continuous and heavy concentrations, being an Italian rugby player or a member of the armed services of the USA. Very recent research [7], however, does confirm a considerable amount of anecdotal evidence that high physical activity levels is associated with the onset of MND. The researchers point out that this is not a primary cause of MND but along with other predispositions, such as genetic susceptibility, is a contributing factor. The truth is, research that is undertaken has to spread a small amount of money in many directions and as there is little incentive, because of the small numbers of people who contract the disease, the great pharmaceutical companies are not sufficiently motivated to carry out more research.

In the first year after my diagnosis, I read avidly as much as I could about the disease. I was especially interested in what progress was being made to research a cure and I signed up for the MND research blogs, which at that time looked quite promising. There was one particular research project, rather oddly called Brainstorm[8], which seemed to offer the best prospect at the time. It was a collaborative piece of international research between universities in the USA, the UK, the Netherlands and Israel. Its focus was on the use of regrowing motor neurones through the use of stem cell technology. There had been a promising start with a small-scale pilot project that established its acceptability from a medical ethics point of view and that it would not create adverse side effects. The next stage was to undertake a doubleblind trial with a much larger sample. Unfortunately, this was not to start until October in 2016 and was due to produce some results by June the following year. Even if the pilot research were positive, I became aware that it would be many years later before it was ready to be rolled out for effective use. Other research at the time, I noticed, was looking at ways of slowing up the progress of the disease and how to diagnose it more effectively. There was quite a lot of focus on isolating individual genes, which might explain the hereditary condition of MND, that is responsible for probably less than 10% of sufferers, or so it was thought at the time; the most recent thinking now is that many more people may have a genetic predisposition to the disease that could be triggered by various environmental factors. Progress in trying to establish exactly what are the causes of MND is painfully slow and elusive, though there is general agreement there is no one single cause. There are a number of suggestive correlations, referred to earlier, but to date there is no conclusive scientific evidence providing an explanation for any of these.

At the time I started to examine these research projects, there seemed to be some large-scale and promising possibilities that were well funded. Since then, however, much of the research seems to have become small-scale, providing funds for individual PhD students, which, whilst important, is quite peripheral to what I consider to be the more important aims in establishing its causes and, most crucial of all, a cure. I think what has happened is that the funds have predominantly diminished since the success of the Ice Bucket Challenge[9], which not only educated many people about the disease but also provided substantial funds. Before the challenge, the average amount of money raised was £200,000 a week; during the week August 22nd to the 28th in 2014 it went up to £2.4 million.

I no longer now invest much hope in being able to benefit from medical research. The timescale over which research occurs no longer favours me so even if there were a miraculous breakthrough in the near future it would take years of testing and field trialling to come to fruition. It is a rare condition with only about 5000 sufferers in the UK[10] alive at any one time. Research is simply not going to be profitable enough.

There is no effective treatment for MND, despite claims made on the Internet by unscrupulous clinics and individuals. The only tried and tested one is Riluzole, that does nothing more than slow the progression rate down by three months. I was prescribed this medication when I was diagnosed, but after three weeks, having reached a full dosage, I was in a far worse state than before. I was sleeping almost throughout the day and experiencing bouts of nausea. Apparently this is a known side effect. Furthermore, I had to provide a blood sample every month to measure any potential damage to my kidneys and liver from the medication. I therefore concluded the benefit was hardly worth the cost and stopped taking the drug, after which my quality-of-life rapidly improved. The only other treatment for MND is palliative care, which embraces a whole range of services and people. I was placed under a palliative consultant, with a specialism in MND who has supervised me ever since the first few months after I saw a neurologist at the Queen Elizabeth Hospital, Birmingham.

Pick your poison

Before I was officially diagnosed, I spent a great deal of time on the Internet researching my symptoms trying to find out what possible illness I had. In addition to MND, and its variants, which I have referred to, two other conditions suggested themselves. These were Muscular Sclerosis and Muscular Dystrophy. When I knew there was something seriously wrong with me, but before diagnosis, I sometimes wished it would be one of these rather than what it was. Having got to know more about these diseases, I don't think that anymore and I certainly don't wish to insult anyone who suffers from them.

Muscular Sclerosis

MS[11] affects the muscle groups just like MND but for a different reason. The myelin sheaths which surround the nerves in the central nervous system deteriorate interfering with the signal to them from the brain. Depending on the kind of MS a person has, will determine the rate of progression and decay. MS is not regarded as a terminal disease, although it may shorten life by an average of seven years. There are also treatments available to ameliorate significantly the effect of some forms of MS. It is a much more frequent condition than MND with 30 to 40 people per 100,000 in the population, which is currently the approximate number of sufferers today in the UK. The more serious stages of MS can be excessively pernicious, as effectively it is an anti-autoimmune illness that affects the bowels, sexual function as well as the different muscle groups. Similar to MND, the causes of MS are not known and it is conjectured that it is a result of a combination of genetic and environmental factors. The progression of the disease also various enormously with individuals. Some types of MS may remain stable for a long time after which a relapse may occur to a more serious level and then there may be a recovery period.

Muscular Dystrophy

There are about six different types of muscular dystrophy (MD) all of which will affect the muscles of various parts of the body by weakening them. It is a genetic mutation which causes it. The most prevalent is Duchenne MD which starts in childhood and usually means a shortened lifespan, affecting boys more frequently than girls. Adults who contract MD are likely to do so in their 40s and 50s and this is called Yotnin MD. This is not usually terminal nor life shortening, although the sufferer maybe prone to greater infection, particularly from pneumonia. In children it is an especially distressing disease because of the rapid immobility that it causes and not infrequently leads to death in the first few years.

Parkinson's Disease

Parkinson's disease results from the dying of cells in a certain part of the brain that produce dopamine. Dopamine regulates many of our movements and therefore sufferers show characteristic signs of handshaking, weariness and stiffness of limbs, anxiety, loss of memory and general lack of social and physical confidence and competence. It usually occurs after the age of 50 years, but may occur earlier. There are a number of successful treatments now to slow up the progress of Parkinson's but there is no outright cure.

Huntingdon's Disease

Huntingdon's disease[12] is an inherited genetic disorder of the nervous system and tissues. The onset is usually between the ages of 30 and 50 years but it can occur earlier in a juvenile form. There is no cure for it and, as with other neurological conditions, its progression and course are individual to the person. It is likely to affect the muscle system i.e. movement, cognitive function and emotional behaviour. It is another pernicious disease and so commentators have likened it to having MND, MS and Dementia at the same time.

Chapter 5

Third Stage of My MND Journey

Transition to Hoist

In October 2016 I had a very bad cold, bordering on influenza. I was extraordinarily lucky that it didn't settle on my chest and give me a bronchial infection, which is the great risk for someone in my condition and declining ability. However, there was a consequence because it drained me of so much energy it finally put paid to the last reserves in my legs that had until then allowed me to transfer from chair or bed using my power chair. It was a very tricky and risky technique of transfer whereby I shuffled forward on my power chair balancing precariously on the upraised edge. I was then able to place my feet on the ground with straight legs and with my arms on the edge of the bed or chair I wanted to transfer into complete the movement successfully. Then I had sufficient strength to stand and turn into it. It was only a matter of time really before I either fell or I was unable to muster the strength in my legs for this manoeuvre. Fortunately, the Handling and Moving Occupational Therapist had provided us with a hoist three months before in the event of any difficulties that might develop, as we all knew they would eventually. We had also practised using the sling to transfer into it and we were used to seeing it there. We tucked it away at the bottom of the bed where it was not an intrusion and we could retain as much normality in the room as possible so it didn't resemble a hospital room. Nevertheless, it was a significant psychological blow and I was quite depressed for a few days although that had probably also been brought on by the illness.

Carol and I were still sharing a king-sized bed with a profile facility on my half. Now, although I could still just about perch on the edge of the bed, I had to get used to lying flat and being rolled from side to side for a sling to be fitted. In the mornings, therefore, I am hoisted out of bed and into a shower chair where I am taken to the wet room and placed over the toilet bowl. The urine bottle is perched in front of me on the chair, allowing me a degree of privacy on the loo after which I shout for the carers to enter and shower or wash me. After this procedure, I am wheeled outside where I am re-hoisted into the air for the return to my chair or bed. Normally, the practice is to return the patient to lie on the bed, dress them and then put the sling back on them for re-hoisting. All of this takes a considerable amount of time and is quite tedious. However, I had picked up a very useful tip from the hospice that I attended, that cut out the necessity of having to use the bed again. This ingenious procedure requires underwear and trousers to be pulled over the sling in the hoist and then removed after the transfer. It works wonderfully and I have taught it to many carers who watch at first incredulously but after which they adopt it readily. Using the hoist isn't pleasant but I have grown used to it and anyway there is no alternative. It does, of course, signify for people like me yet another nail in the coffin, but after a week or two it becomes normalised.

Toileting

One of the most difficult things to get used to, which applies to anyone who is wheelchair-bound and doesn't have upper body strength, is to rely on someone to help you go to the toilet. For a male, urination is a fairly straightforward process so long as one has a suitably designed urine bottle i.e. long enough and large enough. Be that as it may, there is still the obstacle of bashful bladder syndrome, or BBS for short. In the privacy of the wet room, there is no problem but when one is in one's chair, it is quite another matter. Although it may be common practice for men to share public urinals in Western culture, I, and I suspect many other men, have always found it difficult to use such facilities and where possible have always sought the privacy of a cubicle. It was a nightmare for me when I had to spend nine days in a Nursing Home for respite care last year because there were well over 20 different carers/nurses, mostly female, with whom I came into contact and from whom I required help. Various ploys were used such as running water, talking about the weather or anything that was normal just to relieve the nervous anxiety, but when you have to go you have to go! It's curious how one gets used to some individuals more than others. For instance, the person with whom I had the most difficulty was a male nurse! He was a lovely, gentle person and excellent nurse but I just couldn't do it.

I suppose many people who have been in hospital for an operation have had to use a bedpan. Fortunately, I haven't but I've heard how difficult it can be to use one especially when it is compounded by medically induced constipation from painkillers so that laxatives and bowel irrigation have to be used. I do take morphine and I therefore have to manage this negative effect of the drug by using a recommended laxative. The most difficult and personally demeaning aspect of opening one's bowels, however, is having to rely on someone to clean one up. Here again, the amazing human capacity for routine and normalisation kicks in after a while so that it becomes an acceptable part of the daily routine. I think good carers show their value when they are capable of putting people at their ease in these circumstances. It is a lot to get used to in a short period of time though i.e. losing one's ability to walk at all, using a hoist, and being toileted by people you hardly know.

Eating and Drinking

For 18 months following diagnosis, I was still able to use a knife and fork after a certain fashion but by the end of the second year I had neither the finger nor arm strength to do this. It was a gradual transition from using a large handled fork or spoon to not being able to lift one at all. I became totally dependent on someone to feed me or lift a glass from which to sip using a straw. Another Rubicon was crossed. I have even got used to being fed in public now and, whilst I prefer to drink wine directly from the glass, I'm very happy to suck half a pint of beer through a straw, which I can do remarkably quickly. However, gone are the days when I could linger over a good quality wine, sniffing it, rolling it around in my hands and then sucking in a mouthful to tantalise the tastebuds even further. It is much more functional now and that's one reason why I barely consume more than one glass of wine at dinner.

Sometimes I'm tempted to try and use a straw and sip from a glass of water whilst still using my ventilator but I have to be careful. There have been a number of occasions when the oesophagus didn't respond quickly enough leading to unpleasant choking attacks. Obviously, whilst eating I cannot wear my NIV and it now becomes a race before I run out of breath to finish my meal, especially in the evenings when I am more tired. Until recently, Carol always ate alongside me in order to retain that level of normality which we have both prized since I began to deteriorate but which cannot always be sustained. It makes socialising difficult as people like to linger over their food and enjoy the dinner table conversation, all of which together has become too difficult for me. Consequently,

I tend to eat first and then Carol will retrieve her meal from the oven. Sometimes I can only get through half my dish before I need my ventilator replaced, when Carol will then be able to start her meal and we eat in relays. Remarkably, I am still able to swallow and chew my food, though I have noticed I have to be careful of my posture in the chair when it seems as though food has got stuck in my gullet because of the lack of stomach muscles, which provided the strength for a straight conduit. The balance of the quality of my life therefore remains positive whilst I can do this. I have made it very clear right from the start, however, that when I can no longer swallow I will not accept a PEG.

Sleeping

Until about six months ago, I very much looked forward to going to bed at night when I could usually rely on a good night's sleep. This is no longer the case and it is becoming increasingly problematic as I wake up sometimes after only an hour and need turning on my side or my back, the only two positions available to me. It must be something to do with my weakened muscles that make it more and more uncomfortable to sleep soundly. I am aware of aching joints in my shoulders or knees when I have spent some time sleeping on my right side. I'm not able to sleep on my left side which appears now to be too weak to hold me without considerable discomfort and pain. If I'm lucky, I can go nearly 3 hours in this position and then I wake up requiring to be moved. If I'm on my back, then I may wake up with cramps in one of my calves. But sometimes it is not easy to identify why I've suddenly woken up. There are the obvious factors to do with feeling thirsty, when I will then obtain some sips of water with the help of my carer, or because I am too hot or too cold. My personal temperature regimen seems to be a lot more sensitive to variations in temperature. I become either excessively overheated or my core body temperature drops so low I need hot water bottles and extra blankets to warm me up again. This is usually because I have become imperceptibly cooler during the evening to a point when I am not able to regenerate my own heat.

I have discussed the sleeping difficulties with my consultant who has prescribed sleeping tablets and morphine (Oramorph) to relieve my discomfort. I found that the first two sleeping tablets I took stopped being effective after a few days and usually gave me a headache. I also discontinued using the liquid morphine because of the problems with constipation so the consultant prescribed a slow release dosage which seems to be working though its potency has definitely diminished. For some months, we thought the problem could be to do with the bed I was in and so various mattresses were tried and discarded. Eventually we obtained a hospital bed with an air mattress that is absolutely wonderful. There are certain times when it feels as though I am being embraced gently and warmly by someone - all of which is provided by the NHS! But it now means that Carol and I no longer share a bed. It is a further step away from normality and the intimacy we have always been used to for so many years together.

Alarms

These days I require constant attendance, which is usually undertaken by either Carol or the carers. I still have a reasonably strong voice, which is another unusual feature of my particular journey with MND, 80% of sufferers losing the ability to speak. It is just as well because I can't use a keyboard, and except for a jellybean button I can press, I can't use my hands to communicate. So, if I want anything I must call for it.

Until six months ago, I used an alarm which could be activated by a pendant switch or a jellybean button. This has served me well for over two years but now my hands and arms are too weak to use these devices without adaptation. I now have an extraordinary device known as a Swan neck, which Carol and I refer to as ET because of its rather strange futuristic design. This clamps onto the side of my bed stretching onto the mattress so that I can just about operate it with the back of my hand, as it is very sensitive. When I am working on my computer, which is most of the day, I now have a mounted pedestal with the activation button surmounted by a marmalade lid that provides further coverage so that I can normally hit it with the back of my hand, unless my hand has fallen off its perch on the lap table. A backup we use, which has become absolutely essential, is a baby-com that we bought from the local market and picks up the quietest of noises. The problem with this, however, is its limited range and if anyone is listening to the radio in the kitchen, they won't hear me. All of these devices and Heath Robinson adaptations allow whoever is attending me to get on with something else and I can do my own thing too. I'm not used to people waiting on me hand and foot and I also want to be able to be in control of whatever I'm doing, so it is good to have a degree of independence that the voice activation software on my computer allows me and to get help and support via the alarm should I need it.

I have recently received some wonderful new equipment which gives me greater control over my environment. An organisation called Access to Communications Technology, at the request of social services, have provided me with a device which enables me to switch the TV on and off, select programmes, answer and make telephone calls, and even switch on a lamp or fan by using it. It operates on a menu system which is connected by infrared to the jellybean button.What did people like me do before this wonderful technology became available?

My Daily Life

I am largely confined to my riser recliner chair during the day and as it has been a harsh winter this year and really too cold to venture out very much in my power wheelchair, I have been largely housebound. The weather is slowly improving and I have been outside during the last two weeks. Grabbing a few hours in the sun with temperatures of 25°C has been transforming. Sharing the Quarry Park in Shrewsbury with all the town's students made me feel human again. I hadn't been out for quite a few weeks and within that time the strength in my hand had noticeably deteriorated so that I found it difficult to steer and to exert pressure for very long. We had a rear set of controls fitted for just this eventuality about eight months ago and now Carol had to use it in earnest. I found this extremely dispiriting because of the loss of control. I know Carol will always encourage me to go outside when the weather is suitable, even if it is just to sit in the sun on the patio, admiring the work she has done in the garden. But I find it increasingly tiring to get into the power chair even though I now have an in situ sling which I don't have to remove making life much easier. I hope we can continue to make our little visits to town and the local hostelries where we can enjoy some lunch for some time to come yet. We live in a very beautiful part of the country and feeling the fresh air on my cheeks reminds me of how good it is to be alive.

I have a number of friends who visit when we sit chatting about where we used to work, politics or the family. When I'm on my own during the day I spend time writing, reading, learning languages or listening to music. I have a wonderful little system, a hard disk, which allows me to store my music from the computer or download it from the Internet and to control it via Wi-Fi from my Apple Air Mac. But I wouldn't be able to do any of this without a wonderful piece of dictation software called Dragon Professional, which I was able to get with the help of Social Services also from Access to Communication and Technology. It allows me to navigate between applications and write books. It has quite literally been my lifeline to the world and contributes enormously to my current quality of life.

Chapter 6

Medics, Nurses, Other Professionals and Carers

Medics

The MND Association is aware that because the disease is quite rare many doctors don't actually come across it either during training or later in their careers. Consequently, it provides a great deal of advice for both professionals and patients. Furthermore, MND is not easy to diagnose and tests

81

are carried out to eliminate other possible conditions which can be identified, by, for example, blood tests and spinal marrow tests. Therefore, GPs don't have it on their radar from the start when a patient visits them with a certain problem and much time may be lost by sending them to an inappropriate consultant, which is what happened in my case. One could argue there should be much greater awareness amongst GPs of the range of confusing and overlapping neurological conditions that can affect their patients. I know each individual disease has its own organisation to do just this to provide that information on request, but I wonder whether in the busy, frenetic reality of primary care practice this can often get sidelined? Should it not be a part of every doctor's training? Perhaps it is, but does this go beyond textbook knowledge to actual practice? When I was in the hospital at Stoke, I was visited by an internee who came specifically to talk to me and looked me over as though I was some strange, exotic beast that he'd heard about but never seen. I was a little cruel to him because when he asked whether there was anything he could do for me, I said, 'Yes please, cure me. '

The group of doctors who deal with conditions like mine are neurologists. This is a highly specialised and high status part of the medical profession. I understand from a neurologist friend, that they only take the brightest and the best. As the tests that are used for some of the conditions, like MND, are not simply a matter of reading instruments but require the exercise of clinical observations, combined with experience, this claim may well be true. All doctors, of course, should listen to the patient's history as well as make use of their visual faculties. My experience suggests that this is often restricted by time or over specialisation in their own field that leaves them blinkered to other possibilities. One GP I visited, when I was concerned about the pain in my back and the difficulties with climbing hills, asked me to remove my trousers and lie on his couch. After studying me for a few minutes, he was quite convinced that one thigh looked thinner than the other. He then proceeded to take a tape measure from his drawer putting it around each thigh, confirming his erudite suspicions. He then referred me to the orthopaedics Department of the local hospital. Why he did this, I have no idea. Eventually, I received an appointment to attend the Department when I saw the Consultant briefly who said I should have an x-ray and wait for the result. Two hours later, I was again on the couch of the specialist who said he couldn't see anything wrong from the x-rays and that it would be a good idea to refer me for an MRI. After six weeks I duly attended for the MRI test and eventually once again turned up on the same couch with the same Consultant. This time he looked at my legs again and asked whether I cycled, which I did. He seemed to be quite impressed by the size of my thighs! After a brief chat, he then said he could detect nothing on the MRI scans and seemed to be on the point of dismissing me when I repeated that there was indeed a problem because I was experiencing difficulties still with climbing hills. He considered this for a few moments and then suggested I be referred to physiology for further checks. The outcome of this exercise was that I was enrolled on the six-week muscle strengthening physiotherapy programme provided at the hospital. Well, I thought, this is good, at least something is happening and no doubt all will be cleared up in the not too distant future. I successfully passed the physiotherapy training course at the end of which I saw a senior physiotherapist who said that everything was now finished as far as they were concerned because there was nothing more they could do. Again, I repeated to her that I was no better, my symptoms had not disappeared and were getting worse. The only thing she could suggest was that I refer back to the orthopaedic consultant, though she did mention the possibility of referral to a neurologist. That was the first time this course of action had been suggested. I agreed to all of this, but nothing came of the neurology reference except a reference back once more to orthopaedics. After another MRI scan, the Orthopaedic Consultant finally said I should be referred to a neurologist.

I was now becoming quite disheartened by the NHS's treatment of me. As a member of the immediate post-war generation, I was brought up to have an almost blind faith in the quality and provision of the NHS. I had absolute confidence that the service would come through and provide me with whatever I needed. Now that I really needed them, for the first time in my life, I was to discover that that faith was misplaced. First of all, I had to learn that one could not just sit back and wait for the service to be provided, even for something as simple as an appointment with an appropriate consultant. Despite having been told that I was being referred to a neurologist, months went by without hearing anything. When I contacted the hospital to speak to the secretary of the only permanent neurologist in the county, I discovered there was a waiting list that I didn't appear to be on. I went back to my GP who said he would write to ensure that I was. Again, months went by and I heard nothing. I did, however, discover when I rang the Consultant's secretary that I was at last on the list, but there were two or three other names in front of me. Over the next few months, I discovered there was always two or three in front of me! In the end, I implored my GP, who was new to the practice – a part-time locum who was eventually taken on full-time, I'm glad to say - to do something. He took my position seriously, the first time I felt anyone had, was as concerned as I was at my rapid loss of weight and said he would organise an out of area appointment. This came through within a month and I eventually saw a neurologist in Sandwell who was working from the Queen Elizabeth's Hospital in Birmingham. This was in August. It was, however, another two months before I was notified to attend for tests at QE in Birmingham. These were electrical tests which confirmed I had some serious neurological condition demanding urgent investigation. Within a week, I received an appointment at Queen Elizabeth's with an MND specialist neurologist.

Why the delay? According to the Association of British Neurologists[13] there is a severe shortage of neurologists in the UK. Apparently, the ratio is 1: 150,000 people, whereas in the rest of Europe that ratio is only 1:25,000. When the admissions to hospital for acute neurological treatments range from 10 to 20% of the total around the country, one has to ask why there are so few neurologists? There are many people suffering from TIAs and epilepsy as well as those conditions I have already mentioned above who clearly need a regular daily service. But the survey by the ABN also reveals that there is very uneven provision around the country with only 43% of general hospitals able to offer a daily regular service from a neurologist. In Shropshire, if the European average was adopted, there would be 14 neurologists in the area instead of the current one full-time and one or two extra available on a part-time basis. No wonder I got the runaround.

Professions Allied to Medicine

Despite there being an insufficiency of neurologists in Shropshire, the support services for MND patients are excellent and I would guess are one of the best in the country. A few months after being diagnosed at QE in Birmingham, I received one visit from one of the dedicated MND nurses there and attended a further clinic, when I saw another neurologist. He told me it was not essential to continue attending at Birmingham, quite a distance from where I live, and I could be referred to the local service. As Birmingham serves a large population with a heavy demand on its services, obvious from the packed clinics that I'd attended, Carol and I thought it would be better to go local. Shropshire does have a dedicated MND support worker but it also has a Palliative Care Consultant based at the local hospice who has a specialism in MND. I've been told that it was the ex-head of the neurology service, Simon Nightingale, who still practises on a private part-time, who was responsible for setting up this service. It seems to have gone from strength to strength. There is excellent liaison between all members of the team, which includes consultants and nurses at the Royal North Staffordshire Hospital in Newcastle-under-Lyme and all other health practitioners, as and when they are needed. The palliative care consultant takes a leading role in this. She holds clinics about every six weeks and now that I need it, provides a home visit service too. The dedicated MND support worker answers directly to her and is now located in the same building. I've heard that in some counties there is no such support worker and no one to ensure the provision of good advice and information and top-level liaison between all health contributors. It must be extremely distressful for those MND sufferers who are having to cope at the same time with what is a terrible illness, for which, according to the MND Association's guidelines, a total team support is essential. They should not have to suffer such an uneven and patchwork provision, subject to a postal code lottery.

So, who are members of the support team and why are they so important? First and foremost, it is important to ensure that the GP is on board. I would argue this should be a dedicated person who knows you, has researched and is informed about the condition and with whom other members of the team are in contact. At my own surgery, this wasn't initially the case because of the practice, introduced in recent years, of seeing any doctor who was available. I find this totally unacceptable given what I said earlier about the paucity of knowledge in the medical profession of the illness. I was very fortunate to have a GP, new to the surgery, who was prepared to get to know me and my wife and was concerned just as much about her health as mine. It is easy to think in the early stages following diagnosis that any manifestation of being unwell is a consequence of MND, but of course that is not always the case. I know I suffer from arthritic gout and have done for over 15 years but it is not caused by the disease though it may accentuate the symptoms, as it did for me. There is always the risk of various infections, particularly bronchial ones, which could become life threatening. Then, if one is on riluzole, the only medicine which may slowdown the progression of the disease, it is necessary to have regular blood tests because of the damage this medication can inflict on the liver and kidneys. But it has been exceptional for me to visit the GP's surgery and in the past three years I would say I've only had to contact the

GP two or three times. Partly, this is because any medication that is required has been prescribed initially by the Palliative Care Consultant, who is always ready and available to discuss MND and other possible complications.

There are also a host of other people and services who have become indispensable from time to time. In the first year, I periodically attended a physiotherapist at the hospital who could supply equipment such as wheelchairs and Zimmer frames. She was also available at the end of the telephone to advise about muscular cramps and whatever exercise might be suitable. However, services from a physiotherapist are quite limited for someone with MND because there is nothing that can be done to stop the weakening of the muscles -exercises to strengthen muscles are not possible and may actually be injurious. However, if one is suffering from complete loss of control of the neck or leg, for example from drop foot, then there is equipment that can be provided. The other key person with whom Carol and I have built up a tremendous relationship, who has provided a whole range of equipment and advice, is the Occupational Therapist. She has been the gateway to obtaining ramps, a hoist, shower chair, a rise and recline chair, alarm buttons, a hospital bed and even a bidet. I also must not forget Wheelchair Services who provide and maintain the all-important power chair, who have been excellent in keeping me on the road and out and about.

Other people with whom we have come into contact and who have provided invaluable support are, for want of a better phrase, the Moving and Handling Lady who provided us with practical demonstrations on how to use the hoist and the accompanying sling. She was also able to advise on the safest way of moving me in bed. In the last six months I've also been plagued by oedema or swelling of the feet and lower legs as a result of increased immobility. The Palliative Care Consultant instructed District Nurses to attend in order to provide me with compression stockings of the sort one has in hospitals. At first, it was tantamount to mediaeval torture and felt like my feet were being broken each time the stockings were fitted. I subsequently learned they were causing more harm than good because they were too strong and could have caused the swelling to migrate up my body! Fortunately, one of the District Nurses had just been on a training course on the use of a completely new design of stocking which wraps around the legs and feet by being peeled on and held in place by velcro. These have transformed the whole painful exercise and it seems to have had some effect.

The Hospice

The Severn Hospice provides a marvellous palliative care service employing a whole range of staff from end-of-life nurses, occupational therapists, social workers, consultants, and complementary therapists providing aromatherapy and a range of different massages. It's extraordinary that were it not for the energy and foresight of one individual nurse this hospice would not have been opened in 1989. As with all hospices, it is only funded voluntarily yet provides such an important and essential service to the whole community. It's crazy that they are not incorporated into the NHS. I attended a day unit for 18 months until I decided I didn't require it because

I was receiving so much care at home. However, I value the time I spent there, and all the wonderful people I met including patients, volunteers and staff. The staff there were responsible for ensuring that I received full CHC funding i.e. continuous health care without which the home care package I now receive would not have been possible because at a cost currently in excess of £5000 a month it is well beyond our resources to provide.

My MND coordinator had advised us that we should apply for CHC funding as soon as possible as we would be requiring increasing amounts of care in future. She was absolutely right. She had arranged for a social worker to interview us and help us complete the complicated and rather lengthy application form. This particular Social Worker did not give us the service that we were experiencing from the rest of the team. For example, she took two forms out of her briefcase and made cursory references to one of them saying that that was unlikely to be relevant! It was in fact the most crucial form of the two but she had decided that it didn't apply to me when it most certainly did. She seemed to be in a hurry looking at her watch the whole time and this was because, it was subsequently revealed, she had ordered a taxi for her to be picked up after an hour since she was not a car user. She concluded the interview when there was a honking outside, which was her taxi. Job done and time to go, as far as she was concerned. I don't think I quite realised at the time how important this form filling was because then I was receiving little if any formal care. Carol was my sole carer except for the visits to the hospice. The final travesty was when this social worker leaned over towards me and tapping me on my knee said, 'Keep up your strength.' She then disappeared. Carol was beside herself with rage and I was quite bemused. Did she not know what my condition was? Had she not even done that basic preparation for her visit? Later we realised, it begged the question as to how she could possibly have assisted us with this application. The MND coordinator herself was incandescent although she tried to keep it to herself as a good professional. We ought really to have complained about the Social Worker but we didn't because there were so many other things we were having to do and come to terms with. Eventually, our MND coordinator asked the staff at the hospice to begin the process all over again and one of the senior nurses and social workers assisted me to do that. It was finally completed by one of the nurse administrators at the Funding Council, who gave us excellent advice and in the end we received full funding to which we were absolutely entitled. I wonder how many other people with MND have not been able to access CHC funding because of a similar experience to that which we had at the beginning?

Carers

When one reaches a certain stage, when all or most of the equipment has been provided, then the most important service of all is needed. I'm referring to the official packages of care in addition to the key care one ideally receives informally from one's spouse or partner. The unofficial care will, of course, have been provided from the point of diagnosis if not before. In my case, the need for extra care increased almost imperceptibly until a tipping point when it became obvious that extra help was required. Until then, I know the insidiously increasing demands I placed on Carol began to weigh her down. It's hard work pushing a manual wheelchair, making all the meals, ensuring there are clean clothes every day, keeping up with the house cleaning and whenever we entertained, being the chief cook and bottle washer as well as hostess. It helped to obtain a power chair and when one friend offered to prepare meals that we could place in the freezer, we jumped at it. The best thing that friends can do to help is often the small practical jobs which are often overlooked. But many of our friends have been only too willing to give their time and provide all sorts of assistance when required.

Initially, I didn't require a lot of external help and the first carer came in two days a week only for an hour in the mornings as I could get out of bed, wash and dress myself. But, as time went by, I relied increasingly on carers to do all of this, provide me with food and eventually to toilet me as well as helping me to take medicines and eat my food. I also require turning every two or three hours either in the chair or in bed every night. Carers provide all this kind of service but there are many different levels and quality of service and one is very much at the mercy of the particular agency one is contracted with. It is certainly a Rubicon to cross when one realises one has to invite carers into one's home, invading one's privacy and confirming once again there is no going back, that this disease carries on relentlessly debilitating one.

At the beginning, I was lucky because I had an excellent carer who was experienced, dedicated and interesting to talk to. However, I was to learn that not all carers are   as committed as he was. It is astonishing that there are not more who strive to do as little as possible and are slipshod in their approach to their work. Almost all of them are on zero hour contracts and paid the minimum possible wage that is currently £8.05 p an hour. What's more, if they are paid for travel, the rate is generally 20p a mile. The most iniquitous part of their so-called contracts is that there is no payment for travelling time, so the carer may be paid 40 hours a week for actual contact time with the client, or the service user in their lingo, but they will invariably have additional time when they must travel between calls. If they have an accumulation of many small jobs of say 30 minutes or an hour, they are likely to spend another 20 to 30 hours a week travelling for which they are not paid. Some are luckier because they may have a sitting service of 3 to 6 hours and so the problem of unpaid travel time is not so great. Furthermore, this problem can be compounded when the agency fails to pay the cost of travelling for a month or more and in some cases this may amount to over £100. The first agency I was with was particularly poor in this respect and it led to a lot of disgruntlement with the staff who were always having to chase up what was owed to them. There was one carer who had been asked to travel from Wolverhampton, which is over 20 miles away and with whom it was agreed before he started that he would be paid travel time and costs. He was not paid on time and when the delays became quite lengthy he had no option but to resign. He was told he would have to work four weeks' notice, which he rightly ignored as being on a zero hour contract does not require that. Unfortunately for us, he left two days before he should have and we were left without cover, the burden inevitably falling on Carol. He had gone out of his way to help the agency but as a consequence he was earning so little he was forced to look elsewhere. One week the carers were buzzing with a new source of discontent. They had been told that they should clock in and out every time they made a visit, which is something that had not been properly observed for quite a while, and was picked up by a CQC inspection. However, they were concerned when they were told that should the visit fall short of say a full half hour and it was more than five minutes from the allotted time, they would only be paid for the first 15 minutes.

A further problem in the domiciliary care sector is a high turnover of staff. With increasing demand from a growing elderly, disabled population and more recently a change in government policy introducing a measure to cut bed blocking in hospitals, there is always a clamour for staff. I'm surprised that unions have not exploited the situation yet to improve conditions and incomes, but most of the staff I come across are non-union employees. In such a market workers' wages should be rising and, whilst there was an increase recently to the rather ludicrously named *living wage*, it has benefited few because agencies, certainly the first one I experienced, simply clawed back the increase by methods such as those described above. What has happened, however, that has benefited carers, is the implementation of the EU requirement that even zero hour contract workers should have holiday pay. This, of course, has put increased pressure on those agencies who fail to retain staff. I know of at least three carers I have lost because of the way they were mismanaged and whose experience led them to become disgusted with the way corners were being cut by the agency. All of these people found employment subsequently in residential care and I believe there is a drift into that area because many private care and nursing companies offer staff a proper contract with regular hours without the need to be spending hours on the road going from client to client. The drawback, however, with many residential homes, even the well-run ones, is that they are just understaffed and consequently carers have to rush around from one resident to another, which can often result in a lack of time spent with them forcing much less personal service. Another problem that arises from this perennial shortage of staff is that agencies must be continually training staff and some are not too fussy about ensuring the quality and suitability of such people for care work. It is such a pressured industry that it is not surprising that insensitive, uncaring individuals are recruited sometimes who are prepared to cut corners and not provide clients with a basic level of care and civility that one would expect. I believe the fault here lies in a combination of unscrupulous companies and immoral individuals. It is the worst possible combination for this type of work and yet we are coming to rely on it increasingly for everyone.

There is also a conflict between the different categories of service user/client. Some, like myself, are high maintenance and require a dedicated team of staff who are intelligent, caring and prepared to learn the skills suitable for my needs. I'm lucky that I now have this but it is only recently this has been put in place with the help and support of the CHC nursing administrators. I cannot praise my current agency highly enough and I believe that it is well named as **Home Instead**. Other clients may only require a sitting service when having a chat and making tea are all that is required. Despite this, the carers are paid exactly the same. Sometimes, certain categories of user seem to have been given preferential treatment as with my previous agency when I know that a carer, who was on their way to attend to me, was diverted to another client thus making them an hour or more late. This seemed to arise out of a new, and presumably lucrative contract, the agency had secured for what is known as Re-ablement, which refers to those often elderly hospital patients who are no longer in need of healthcare but cannot look after themselves if they are sent home; that comes under social care. Last year the Government made funds available for this group of people to reduce hospital bed waiting times. This service is not usually intended to be permanent and may only last for a few weeks. Carers informed me that in many cases they were only allocated 15 minutes for such visits -hardly enough time to put one's head round the corner to say hello. I presume what should have happened was that the agency should have recruited additional staff, specially trained for this purpose, rather than plundering staff from their current commitments.

With the first agency I experienced, we hardly ever received a weekly schedule of visits giving the appropriate time and name of staff. When we did finally obtain the schedule with perhaps a day or two to spare, if we were lucky, we noticed staff that were inappropriate to us, whom we had refused in the past, or the times were wrong or there was simply a blank. There was a lack of continuity and stability in the staff whom we could expect and sometimes we simply didn't know whether someone would be turning up or not. If not, this put a great deal of pressure on Carol and contributed to the already considerable burden she was carrying. That is the reason why finally we decided we had to find a new agency that had a good reputation. When we did, this sort of unnecessary anxiety was removed. It has made a huge difference to both of us and I even feel confident enough now with the new team that I can be left for a few days whilst Carol obtains some much-needed respite.

But this hasn't come cheaply and without the help of the local CHC administrators it would not have been possible.

As everyone knows, the care sector is in crisis and in need of reform if we are to give people like me and the growing numbers of elderly and infirm people a decent, civilised life in their twilight years. At the moment, it's very much a postcode lottery with some counties and local authorities having to cut back, often because of government underfunding, on the services they provide in every way and kind. As adult social care tends to be at the bottom of the heap i.e. the Cinderella, this is very worrying. I know of at least one county according to the press i.e. Leicestershire, which has capped the amount it will spend on individuals so that they will have their hours cut without regard for their continuing needs even when they may be suffering from something like MND. This is not a national health service.

Despite the poor wages that carers receive, there are some people who do make money from the care sector. For example, the CEO of the first agency I was with received £157,000 in 2016 to 17 on top of which he received a pension contribution of £15,000 that year. The current agency I'm with doesn't disclose the individual amounts per director, under the small companies regulation, but you can get some idea of the rather lavish sums involved when the accounts reveal that four directors received £672,000 in dividend bonuses in the year 2016 to 17. I don't know what individual managers at the individual branches receive but according to the accounts there are only 43 employees in the company, whereas according to the website there are 800+. Of course, the difference here is between those who are on company contracts and those on zero hour contracts i.e. the actual carers. Caring needs to be recognised as an important, essential profession which requires a vocational commitment the same as any other healthcare professional, yet they remain at the bottom of the wages hierarchy and subject to contracts which require them to work excessive hours without pay. The range of skills and tasks undertaken by my carers are broad and complex and without their dedication I would be far worse off. We need to recognise this huge contribution from an often unsung, neglected and poorly paid (to the extent of exploitation) group of people, the demand for which will continue to grow.

Chapter 7

Assisted Dying - Rights, Ethics and the Law

I had decided I was not going to wait to be engulfed by MND. I was going to take control of how I died, just as I was used to taking control of how I lived. A further incentive for me came after a visit of my wife's cousin whose mother died 18 months previously from MND. Philip is a highly intelligent and sensitive human being. He knew right away that I wanted to talk intimately to him about his mother's final days. Her remains had been interred in a peaceful, idyllic corner of Shropshire and he took me with him one Saturday morning to visit that lovely place. He had been very close to his mother and spent a great deal of time with her at the end. Rita was a kindred spirit: a humanist, cyclist and very liberal in her views. I was surprised when he told me that she had registered with Dignitas[14], though in the end she did not travel there. Nonetheless she had great courage, which enabled her to take control of her own death, albeit with a considerable degree of suffering. I was impressed by her example and emboldened, and after having investigated the service that Dignitas provided, I decided it was right for me too. I paid the €250 for registration and have maintained it annually ever since. The subsequent annual fee is lower at approximately €70. This did make me feel better and it was a step in the direction in which I wanted to go, even though I was not sure then, and I'm still not sure now, whether I will actually make that journey to Switzerland. I hope I don't have to.

When I told my Palliative Care Consultant about my decision to register with Dignitas, she informed me that I could take control by choosing to withdraw my ventilator and that there was a well-established procedure for this, which was within the law. It was as if a door had been opened and she now felt able to discuss these issues because I had raised the topic first. I realised that she had been prevented by law from doing this until now, lest she be accused of suggesting how I might kill myself. We began to explore the implications of withdrawing NIV (non-invasive ventilation) and initially I thought this was going to be the answer to all my questions and anxieties regarding end of life. However, the more I analysed it, the more it became clear to me it wasn't quite so straightforward. I even tested the commitment of the Consultant by asking her whether, if I phoned her next week informing her that I wished to withdraw NIV, would she comply with my wishes? She said that, firstly, she would need to discuss with me why I wanted to. Well, really she knew this already so I sensed it was not going to be quite so easy after all. Furthermore, when I asked how long it would take me to die once I came off NIV, it became clear this was an unknown depending on my current usage of the ventilator and it could well take many days and probably weeks during which time I would be given increasing dosages of morphine to control my breathing and reduce the unpleasant effects of gradual suffocation. I knew that I would become increasingly dopey and spend more time sleeping than awake. This is not what I wanted. I want to be completely conscious and compos mentis until the final moments. I also prefer not to die in the hospice but at home, as most people do. The thought of my family and friends visiting me over a possible period of weeks waiting for me to die fills me with horror. It would be awful for them and meaningless for me. I felt I was back to square one again but at least I had the option of going to Switzerland. The problem with this option however is knowing when to go: if I left it too late, I would not be able to travel, but on the other hand, if I were well enough to travel I would still be experiencing a positive quality of life, which I would not want to relinquish. It was at this time, that I became aware of Dignity in Dying(DiD)[15].

I think it must've been June or July in 2016 when I noticed an email from DiD's website calling on anyone who was terminally ill to tell their story for a new campaign they were launching. It referred to the specific way they wanted to change the existing law with the safeguards that assisted dying should be limited to those who are terminally ill with six months to live and fully competent adults who know what they are doing. It would also require the approval of two doctors, a cooling off period of two weeks and the approval of a High Court judge. The safeguards seemed appropriate to me, although I had some questions about the eligibility requirements of the proposed law. Nonetheless, I wrote a brief synopsis of my circumstances and sent it back not really expecting to hear any more. When I did receive a reply enquiring whether I would be prepared to become a lead claimant in a future court case, I thought about it once more in depth and discussed it with Carol with whom I had discussed the registration at Dignitas. Although it was emotionally painful for her, she supported me if that's what I wanted to do. It was not clear at that stage that I would become the lead claimant because there was someone else in the frame but as it turned out they were later deemed not suitable.

I had been angry and frightened when I was first diagnosed. I felt powerless because there was no treatment, only relief from symptoms; it was terminal, which meant I was simply going to continue to decline until death. I remember saying to a good friend of mine, whose wife had died of breast cancer after a brave struggle with it over 10 years,
"I don't know whether I can live with this." It was a statement of despair rather than anything else. He looked at me matter-of-factly, behind which lay so many years of suffering, and said, "You have to. There is no option."
We neither of us made reference to, or even thought of I believe, at that time, the option of suicide. He had spent years fighting with his wife to cling to life so that they and their young family could be together for as long as possible. But now I no longer felt powerless; I was taking control of how and when I should die. I felt empowered and far from depressed.

102

At the moment of his liberation, Prometheus is chained again. Through this long night of the soul, as one Christian Medieval mystic has called it, I came to myself. I saw that I was in control of my destiny, if only I had the willpower.

Over the next few months we were vetted. It was done in a very friendly and professional way. Carol and I were also being inducted into the specific form of assisted dying that the campaign group was seeking to introduce. This was based on the Oregon model in the USA, which has been in force since 1997. Assisted dying is a term that is meant to apply to those who are expected to die within six months. It is, therefore, applied to people who are terminally ill and not specifically to those who are chronically sick who may well be experiencing considerable pain and discomfort but whose condition will not lead to death in a short period of time. The term, which is used to refer to these people who wish to end their lives with help from others, is assisted suicide. There are many people who fall into this category and there are countries such as Holland and Belgium, which have passed laws to allow this. I have a great deal of sympathy for such people and do believe that they should have the right to end their lives if they are fully mentally competent and that is their settled wish. Indeed, this was my starting point but the two charming individuals, with whom we established a good rapport over a number of months, carefully outlined why it was their goal to change the law in Britain in order to allow assisted dying. Firstly, it would provide clearer eligibility criteria and safeguards to protect potentially vulnerable people from abuses, for example from rapacious relatives impatiently awaiting an inheritance. Secondly, it was more in line with societal views in the UK, where assisted dying is supported by 80% of the population, compared with lower support for assisted suicide at around 50%. It was also more likely to be accepted in the UK, as the long-term experience from Oregon would be able to be cited in evidence. Finally, a law limited to giving dying people choice and control at the end of life would also be an important bulwark against concerns that any change in the current law would simply open the door to state sanctioned euthanasia.

When reliable evidence[16] shows that over 80% of people in the UK support a change in the law on assisted dying, why is it that Parliamentarians to date have resolutely rejected any proposal to amend the 1961 Suicide Act? Prior to 1961 any attempt to commit suicide was a criminal offence but it came to be realised that this law was too harsh and ignored the many circumstances of personal human suffering that lay behind such acts. It represented the victory of reason and human compassion over the dead hand of historical dogma. In particular, it signalled the end of the primacy of a mediaeval religious value system, which dictates that only God has the right to determine life-and-death. Finally, this change in the 1961 Act demonstrated that the shining star of the European Enlightenment was coming to prevail over human affairs, although it still has a long way to go even after 200 years.

The law has only gone so far, however, because of the very real need to protect people, particularly those who are most vulnerable such as the very old, from criminal abuse and exploitation. Consequently, the law specifically forbids any assistance to suicides from others, which is a criminal offence punishable by a maximum of 14 years imprisonment. Furthermore, it explicitly forbids any help from medical

104

personnel. These concerns remain real today and cannot be ignored, but the blanket prohibition on any assistance can be construed as discriminatory, as for example in my own case, where it is not possible for me to take my own life without assistance from someone else because of my immobility. It also condemns many thousands to an inhumane level of suffering and indignity at the end of their lives. There has to be some way by which this ethical conflict can be resolved. Other legal jurisdictions from six states and Washington DC in the USA, beginning with Oregon, Holland, Belgium and Luxembourg in Europe, and most recently Canada, believe this is possible. It should therefore be possible in the UK and the only reason it isn't thus far is because of the persistence of a conservative traditionalism, which fosters irrational and anti-enlightenment values. Fifty years ago, UK public opinion would probably subscribe to the idea that their lives and actions were properly subject to a higher, divine authority. This is no longer the case. Yet, the lawmakers fail to reflect this. Why? Our political institutions are woefully anachronistic allowing a pre-eminent place for the Church of England with its bishops in the House of Lords who, with only one or two exceptions, continue to oppose any change. Frequently, when you peel away the surface of arguments of many of those opposed to a change in law, you find the reference to the importance of "the sanctity of life". The term sanctity is a religious one and reveals the reliance on a religious perspective with regard to this argument. Specifically, it means that it is not for human beings to make such life-and-death decisions, which are only rightly determined by religious precept and divine authority. Significantly, most of the organisations campaigning against a change in the law try to conceal their religious paradigm in the full knowledge that the

UK is a secular society and such a view carries little weight with a majority of the population

Another institution, which continues to steadfastly reject any compromise, is the medical profession in the form of the British Medical Association[17]. However, this seems to be a recent change of heart since in 2005 its Conference reported the Association was neutral on the matter, though it had been previously opposed. It would seem that since then there has been some very active lobbying by certain groups within and without the Association [18]so that since 2006 their policy has been to oppose the issue. They cite the following grounds:

Permitting assisted dying for some could put vulnerable people at risk of harm.
This point ignores the possibilities of any safeguards, which can be and have been put in place in other societies that approve assisted dying.

Such a change would be contrary to the ethics of clinical practice, as the principal purpose of medicine is to improve patients' quality of life, not to foreshorten it.

There is evidence that illegal involuntary euthanasia occurs in the UK as elsewhere. Furthermore, the practice of double effect, discussed elsewhere, is recognised and accepted by the medical legal profession, which contradicts this argument. (see note 17)

Legalising assisted dying could weaken society's prohibition on killing and undermine the safeguards against non-

voluntary euthanasia. Society could embark on a 'slippery slope' with undesirable consequences.

These points are almost exactly the same as those to be found in the campaign groups opposed to a change in the law and reflect the same kind of unfounded fears. This is unsubstantiated polemic and not what one would expect to find in a respected professional medical body.

For most patients, effective and high quality palliative care can effectively alleviate distressing symptoms associated with the dying process and allay patients' fears.

As I have already pointed out elsewhere, by no means all end-of-life symptoms can be alleviated effectively for everyone. (see note 19)

Only a minority of people wants to end their lives. The rules for the majority should not be changed to accommodate a small group.

This is a curiously unsympathetic statement by a caring body of professionals.

There are a number of inconsistencies in the practice of medicine in this country, which are in sharp contrast to the arguments above. For example, that withdrawal of artificial nutrition and hydration [19], which is a decision taken by individual doctors, is not scrutinised by the courts, unless for cases of people in a persistent vegetative state or with minimal consciousness. The decision to switch off life support ventilation to a patient in a permanent vegetative state does not now require a court order unless there is disagreement between the medical team and parents in the case of children. However, perhaps the most contentious issue is that of **double effect**. This relates to the doctrine and practice of when a physician provides an increased dose of painkillers in order to alleviate suffering but which also has the effect of killing the patient. This is well known, widely practised and legally permissible[20] so long as it is done at the end of life, which is usually meant to be within a few hours and where the main intention is to relieve suffering not to end life. However, when it is known that the second effect will be to cause death, it is a Jesuitical splitting of hairs between the two intentions.

At the same time, there are many doctors and informal groups who support changing the law e.g. Healthcare Professionals for Assisted Dying (HPAD). Other health groups such as the Royal College of Nursing choose to take a neutral stance on the issue. This is also the case with groups that represent MS and MND. One can only suppose the BMA's opposition is a consequence of its professional pride and defensiveness, as revealed in a recent conference of palliative care professionals[21], with one observer commenting that their attitude resembled a highly traditional medical model where 'doctor knows best' and the views of patients who are actually dying were not taken into account. Even amongst palliative care professionals it is recognised that palliative care cannot provide end of life support and freedom from suffering for everyone[22]. Nonetheless there is a widespread view that palliative care and assisted dying are mutually exclusive, though this is not the case in those countries which have assisted dying laws.

It is time now for the majority of people in Britain to be heard and their views respected by politicians. The recent British

Social Attitudes [23] survey reveals that there has been a remarkably consistent level of support for assisted dying since 1995 at around 77% of the population surveyed. It is clear from many surveys, media and social media discourse, as well as many personal conversations I've had with all manner of strangers and friends, that people accept the right enshrined in Article 8 of the human rights legislation of the UN, the ECHR in 1953[24] and incorporated into UK law by the Human Rights Act 1998, that people should have the right of personal autonomy, which means the right to determine the manner of their own deaths and to be provided with assistance thereto should that be necessary:

1. Everyone has the right to respect for his private and family life, his home and his correspondence.

2. There shall be no interference by a public authority with the exercise of this right except such as is in accordance with the law and is necessary in a democratic society in the interests of national security, public safety or the economic well-being of the country, for the prevention of   disorder or crime, for the protection of health or morals, or for the protection of the rights and   freedoms of others.

The Secretary of State for Justice has recently argued[25] that in the case of assisted dying section 2 of the above effectively overrides section 1 because there is no protection for the weak and vulnerable. This position, however, rejects any possibility of including safeguards as proposed by my legal team.

There is another argument, which was eloquently summarised by Lord Sumption in the Supreme Court ruling of *Nicholson and Lamb v Secretary of State for Justice 2014*[26]. In paragraph 228, he outlines the argument that if such a law were passed it would create an overwhelmingly strong indirect influence on the very elderly and vulnerable that they would feel compelled to take this option to prevent them being a burden on others. This appears to be a strong argument but there are a number of problems with it. Firstly, it makes an assumption that this is how people would behave and think. The evidence for such a claim is not provided. It also assumes that people make decisions for one reason and one reason only but this is not an accurate reflection of human behaviour. The fact is that human decision-making is highly complex and the result often of a multitude of factors. The annual reports from Oregon USA provide an evidence base, which shows that there are a lot of reasons lying behind why people choose an assisted death. Year on year the primary reason given is to avoid suffering. It is true that to avoid being a burden is also a reason cited but it is not a primary one. In my own case, and I'm sure in many others, we regret that we are inevitably a burden on our nearest and dearest and society in general. However, by itself it would not be sufficient reason for choosing an assisted death. I am very conscious of wanting to continue to live whilst the balance of my quality-of-life is positive. In fact, I feel a very powerful indirect social pressure to continue to live beyond the point at which I would personally want to. The reason for this is that I don't want to be the agent of overwhelming grief and suffering to those I love most dearly. When the suffering becomes too great and tips it the other way, that'll be the time to make my final decision. Furthermore, the legislation proposed would incorporate safeguards such as the requirement of two doctors to certify that the individual is not clinically depressed, is terminal within six months and has made a rational decision knowing exactly what he or she is doing. In addition, a High Court judge will be required to examine each individual case to ensure there is no undue pressure being exerted by others to influence this decision and it is perfectly feasible for a judge to decide whether the main reason for making such a decision is to rid society of a burden, in which case he could reject the claim.

An extremely strident group[27] of opponents lies amongst various self appointed spokespersons for disabled groups. They are non-elected and therefore cannot be said to represent the vast bulk of disabled people in the UK who, when surveyed, show an overwhelming support (86%) for assisted dying[28]. These self appointed tribunes seem to have an influence quite out of proportion to the views of those whom they claim to represent. Their fiery rhetoric is strengthened by the fact that many of them themselves are disabled. Their fundamental argument seems to be that any concession to the current law would further undermine and devalue disabled people in UK society by implying that any non-abled, unhealthy and chronically sick person should stop being a burden on society by committing suicide. They go even further than this by arguing that any change in the current law will result in a slippery slope at the end of which lies compulsory state euthanasia for the disabled[29]. The fact that there is an absolute chasm between disability and those who are suffering from terminal illness, who will die very soon, is roundly rejected.

NDYUK claim[30] that I am wrong to believe I will experience any suffering at the time of my death. This is quite a remarkable assertion since they cannot know what my own subjective perspective is now or indeed will be at that time. I can only assume they know very little about the course of MND and how people with it suffer at the end of life.

The two main options facing me are: firstly, if I choose to withdraw my ventilating machine, I will experience increased breathlessness and finally suffocation at the very end. Palliative care will consist of medication to ease my breathlessness with morphine and sedatives to relieve any pain. No one knows how long this process will take: it could be from a number of days or weeks or even longer during which time I shall be continually sedated, semiconscious and probably constipated. I do not regard this likely experience as benign and from my point of view will constitute suffering both physically and emotionally. Secondly, if I choose to continue wearing the NIV for as long as possible, then I know I will be in a virtual catatonic state not able to move any of my muscles except my eyes. I regard this situation as comparable to a living hell. These are my views informed by what I have read about MND. Now let us consider an informed, objective perspective taken from the 2016 audit from the Royal College of Physicians reporting on the end of life experience as observed by professional physicians. In their report, they comment that no palliative care, however good, can ensure a 100% peaceful end of life. Their figures reveal the following: pain was controlled in 79%; agitation/delirium in 72%; breathing difficulties in 68%; noisy breathing / death rattle in 62% and nausea/vomiting in 55%. (RCP 2016)

The second claim that is made by Not Dead Yet UK is that "legalising Assisted Suicide will negatively impact on how continuing illness and the lives of disabled people are viewed as a part of contemporary society."(See note 29). This is a non sequitur. How we get from legalising assisted dying for the terminally ill to the general position of non-terminally ill,

112

chronically sick and long-term disabled is not spelt out. To assume that general societal attitudes towards the disabled will be shaped and influenced by a change in the law is just that: an assumption constituting nothing more than a belief, or one might even say prejudice, which is not backed up by any proof. It is a fear manufactured in the heads of those who see themselves as spokespersons for the disabled as a whole. And we know from elsewhere that this sort of rhetoric jumps easily to the assertion that 'State sponsored euthanasia' for the disabled lies at the end of this road. This is fear-mongering of the worst type and is not part of rational discourse.

The third Error which NDYUK make is to insultingly, and perhaps deliberately, conflate the reference to a' dignified' death with the "daily practical, physical and medical assistance to survive" which most disabled people experience. There is a great difference between the latter and the final physical symptoms at the end of life as described above by the RCP, which can be experienced by up to a third of people dying.

The Courts

I wasn't aware that when we began the legal process there would be so many twists and turns, setbacks and disappointments as we navigated our way through the labyrinth of the UK courts. Astonishingly, for the layperson, it was necessary first of all to have a hearing to determine whether we could have a hearing! In legal parlance, this is a Permissions Hearing and a High Court Judge, or as it turned out, three in our case had to decide whether we could go ahead. I was asked to attend this first hearing by the legal team and the campaign group, so that it would be a case revolving around a real person's situation. We had spent the last six months gathering evidence and witness statements from experts, friends and family. I had also taken a test to assess my current mental and psychological state. This is the MME or Mini Mental Examination, which is carried out by a psychiatrist and consists of 30 questions. An emeritus professor from Oxford, no less, carried this out on a voluntary basis and I'm glad to say I passed it! Going to London was no easy matter for me but we recognised how important it was at the start of the case and so I said I would attend this early hearing or a more substantial one later, but not both given the practical and physical difficulties and discomforts of travel. Carol and I decided to drive down in our wheelchair accessible vehicle, but we both recognised we would need help as Carol would have her hands full with me. Fortunately, our good friend Simon stepped into the breach and offered to drive us all the way there and back, whilst he stayed over at his sister's just north of London. I had decided it was too problematic for me to travel by train now, especially as I could not stand or walk at all. We tried to find a disabled hotel in the centre of London but couldn't find one available. I couldn't believe the disabled lobby were intending to appear at the court and had subversively booked up all the available accommodation. But this was just my paranoia! We found a newly built Premier Inn about 40 minutes drive away from the courts and the campaign group, Dignity in Dying, arranged for a disabled taxi from there to the Royal Courts of Justice the following day. One particularly good thing about the accommodation was the availability of a room with a ceiling track hoist. What a marvellous invention! My stepson, Terry, also offered to take time off from work to accompany us as a second carer with his mother. Without all this assistance, it would have been just too much for Carol and I alone.

The following day, a bitterly cold March morning, we arrived outside the Royal Courts of Justice where I was subject to my first mobbing by the press and TV cameras. Surprisingly, I wasn't phased out by this and managed to say something reasonably coherent, probably because I had already given a number of interviews at home since December. Sarah Wootton, the delightful CEO of Dignity in Dying, was also present to meet us for the first time and helped to fend off the feeding frenzy. The court hearing had to be specially arranged in a basement level courtroom to allow me access. I believe we were in courtroom 31, so the large, historic and impressive courtrooms sometimes seen on TV were not accessible for the likes of me. Despite the cosiness, it was all very imposing with lawyers' gowns and wigs everywhere. We stayed for nearly two hours and then decided we would have to get some lunch, and return to the hotel for a much needed rest because we were meeting Baroness Meacher in the afternoon for tea at the House of Lords. This was a real treat and she was a terrific person who was very easy to talk to and was well informed about the case and its background, as one would expect of the chair of the Board of Directors of DiD. It's just as well it wasn't the following day, when the terrorist attack on Westminster Bridge occurred and there was an attempt to enter Parliament, resulting in the killing of a police officer. Subsequently, there was a complete shutdown of Parliament with people not being able to exit or enter for a number of hours.

That evening when I returned home I felt perfectly all right until I had gone to bed and slept a few hours. We were both exhausted but at about 1 AM I woke up with a crushing pain in my chest, aching arms and a headache. I didn't seem to be able to get any relief and given the symptoms we were both concerned that it could be a heart attack. I refused any medical attention and took some indigestion tablets instead because I thought it could be a bad attack of indigestion. However, there was still no relief so I agreed that Carol should ring Shrop Doc, the out of hours emergency telephone number. After a few questions, the telephonist agreed that we would have a call back from a doctor who rang about half an hour later. He decided to send an ambulance and paramedics out as my symptoms had not abated. When they came, I had begun to feel a little better and they checked me out noticing that I wasn't clammy and that the ECG readings were normal. They advised I should take an aspirin after which they wanted to transport me to hospital for a blood test. I point-blank refused to go because I knew I would face hours waiting on a trolley in a hospital corridor. As it was, I was beginning to feel much better and with some more paracetamol, when they left, I did manage to fall off to sleep. In the morning, we contacted the Palliative Care Consultant and explained what had happened and she suggested I obtain some liquid morphine that I could take in any future likely re-occurrence. She said it was possible it was a reflux action after the exhausting three days we had just experienced. From my point of view, I did not want to experience that pain again and although, on the one hand, if it had been something more serious and possibly fatal, I would have regarded that as welcome, but I saw no reason to put up with the horrendous pain of such an attack. There have been one or two re-occurrences but not to the extent of what I'd experienced that night and the liquid morphine, which I now have, has done its job perfectly.

The first news about the Court's decision was a week or so later and it was very disappointing. We were told they had rejected our request for a Judicial Review and we could appeal against this within 36 hours, which we did. It seems an absurdity that this appeal, which has to be submitted so quickly after the first hearing, is heard again, or rather, decided on by the same judges who heard the first hearing. Again, it was rejected but by two to one so that left us a little hope for a further appeal which would take somewhat longer and be decided by different judges. In the end, the new judge took the view that there were certainly grounds for granting a full Judicial Review. Thus, we stumbled over the first hurdle and a full week's hearing, including one day reading time, was eventually scheduled for July. So it seemed, initially at least, that my attendance at the first court hearing had been very much a waste of time, but on reflection it wasn't because of the wide publicity that we obtained. Requests were coming in from radio and TV but we had to refuse most of them because it meant travelling down to London and being in a studio by 7 AM which was completely impossible for us. I don't think people realise unless they've experienced it, the difficulties of getting a severely disabled individual up and prepared to venture outside. From my recliner chair at home to being hoisted into my power chair and then secured in the wheelchair accessible vehicle takes at least three quarters of an hour.

The date for the full Judicial Review hearing, which we had requested to be as soon as possible given my circumstances, was set for the penultimate week in July, the very last working week of the judicial year. The legal team knew then that we were not likely to get a result until the autumn and they were right. In fact it wasn't until early October that we received a judgement which was profoundly disappointing.

The High Court (administrative division) held towards the end of July last year, finally produced its judgment on 5 October. This rejected my claim that the Suicide Act 1961 section 2 is incompatible with Article 8 of the Human Rights Act, undermining my right to personal autonomy i.e. to an assisted death. The rationale for the judgement was particularly disappointing as I explain below but there was one aspect which was favourable. This concerned the issue of whether the courts were competent institutionally to judge on the matter and not leave it to Parliament, which the previous Supreme Court judgment in the Nicklinson case had.

My legal team argued that it was the job of this court to decide whether it was 'practically feasible' for Parliament to devise a scheme whereby people in my situation i.e. of sound mind, over 18 years, terminally ill with not more than six months to live, could be assisted to die without threatening other weak and vulnerable people. The potential threat to those who are 'weak and vulnerable' is the long-standing reason given to support a blanket ban on any form of assisted dying on the grounds that it is not possible to devise any scheme that would protect such a group. My legal team did put forward such a scheme supported by a considerable amount of expert evidence. However, the High Court did not address this question but instead addressed the question of whether Parliament had 'a proper basis' for maintaining the blanket

118

prohibition. Consequently, the High Court did not adequately address the expert witness evidence that we had provided, saying merely that it had referred to some of the evidence that had been provided by us.

The High Court therefore referred to a wide range of evidence, principally provided by opponents of any change to the law, and extended its scope beyond looking at protections for 'the weak and vulnerable ' to the more general arguments of whether (a) it will devalue the sanctity of life principle and, (b) undermine the doctor-patient relationship. This is a surprising focus by the High Court, because neither of these issues were considered to be relevant by the Supreme Court in the Nicklinson case, which is held to be the most recent senior legal authority on the whole issue. Indeed, the High Court produced lengthy quotes and references from organisations like the British Medical Association, the British Geriatrics Society and the organisation, Not Dead Yet, a leading opponent campaign group established by Baroness Campbell, who was also quoted. The weight of evidence selected and the comments and conclusions drawn by the High Court, therefore, were extremely biased and one-sided.

The judgment also dismissed any notion that assisted dying bore any resemblance to the argument surrounding refusal to accept further medical intervention or the withdrawal of such. It took the view that it was not possible to identify when people with MND are in the final six months' stages of life, preferring to accept the view of Baroness Finlay, a palliative care expert (and longstanding campaigner against assisted dying), rather than Prof Barnes, an MND expert, who concludes that whilst prognosis of death is difficult to establish it is not impossible with appropriate clinical experience.

In 2010, following the Debbie Purdy case, the Director of Public Prosecutions introduced guidelines which clarified the question of whether people who helped others to go to Switzerland for assisted dying (or to end their life at home) would not be automatically prosecuted under section 2 of the Suicide Act. Instead, each case would be investigated separately, and where there was evidence that a crime had taken place, prosecutors would then have to decide, taking into account the range of factors in the guidance, whether or not it was in the public interest to prosecute. Broadly speaking, where it is established that people have acted compassionately and not for personal gain or malice, they will not be prosecuted. Many people regard this as exposing 'the weak and vulnerable' to much greater danger of criminal abuse than the safeguards proposed by Lord Falconer under the Assisted Dying Bill, and by my legal team. This important issue was not raised or discussed by the High Court.

Consequently, for many of the reasons outlined above and others, my legal team believed we had a strong case to appeal the judgement. Whether we could proceed to the Appeal Court was decided at a Permissions -hearing on 18 January. We were delighted to hear that we were given full approval to proceed. We had submitted six grounds for appeal, all of which were agreed, and to our surprise the court suggested a seventh ground to be considered as well. The legal team had done an excellent job. These were the grounds the court granted us for appeal:

a. The Divisional Court misdirected itself as to the correct legal test to apply under article 8(2) ECHR ("Ground 1").

b. The Divisional Court adopted a legally flawed approach to the evidence ("Ground 2").

c. The Divisional Court misdirected itself in law as to the approach to take to identifying whether the prohibition contained in section 2(1) SA 1961 is more than "necessary" for the purposes of article 8(2) ECHR ("Ground 3").

d. In light of the errors identified in Grounds 1, 2, and 3 or otherwise, the Divisional Court failed to address significant evidence and material before it relating to the strength of the safeguards proposed by the appellant ("Ground 4").

e. The Divisional Court failed to address the consequence of the accepted presence of "biased decision-making" in treatment refusal decisions ("Ground 5").

f. The Divisional Court misdirected itself as to the approach to take in identifying whether the prohibition in Section 2(1) SA 1961 struck a fair balance between the rights of the appellant and the interests of the community for purposes of article 8(2) ECHR ("Ground 6").

g. The Divisional Court failed to address the legal and moral difference between a request for assistance with dying and a request for euthanasia ("Ground 7").[31]

Lord Chief Justice Underhill agreed that my basic human rights, as defined by article 8 of the United Nations Declaration of Human Rights i.e. the right to personal autonomy and in this case the right to die, had been restricted by the general prohibition ban of section 2 of the UK Suicide Act 1961. The issue that the Divisional Court should have considered was whether this was acceptable by applying what the law refers to as the four tests of proportionality. This means that judges have to weigh up whether the individual infringement of human rights is acceptable when balanced against broader considerations regarding the protection of the weak and vulnerable, current culture and general morals. He found that whilst the first had been done, the court had not given sufficient consideration to the evidence and arguments that my legal team had presented. Indeed, he states above that the Divisional Court had been extremely selective, one may even suggest biased, in presenting only evidence that supported the counterargument i.e. the case supporting the defendant, the Secretary of State for Justice.

Ethics and Rights

'Human rights are the basic rights and freedoms that belong to every person in the world, from birth until death.

They apply regardless of where you are from, what you believe or how you choose to live your life.

They can never be taken away, although they can sometimes be restricted – for example if a person breaks the law, or in the interests of national security.

These basic rights are based on shared values like dignity, fairness, equality, respect and independence.

These values are defined and protected by law. In Britain our human rights are protected by the Human Rights Act 1998. '
(Equality and Human Rights Commission[32])

Ethics refer to the general principles which act as guides to our actions and therefore draw on beliefs which are strongly moulded by culture, ideology and tradition. They are intended to help us to sort out what is right and wrong. They may or may not be supported and enforced by the law and sometimes may in fact clash with it. For example, when the law protects the human rights of LGBT people but certain organisations and/or people choose to discriminate against them. This is precisely one of the core issues at the heart of the assisted dying debate.

As the High Court judgement in our case stated last year, judges are charged with a duty to reinforce the respect for human life. In fact, another way of putting this is that expressed in Article 1 of the Human Rights Act UK 1998, reinforced by the European Convention on Human Rights, 2010, which emphasises the primacy of the right to life:

'SECTION I RIGHTS AND FREEDOMS
ARTICLE 2
Right to life
1. Everyone's right to life shall be protected by law. No one shall be deprived of his life intentionally save in the execution of a sentence of a court following his conviction of a crime for which this penalty is provided by law.
2. Deprivation of life shall not be regarded as indicted in contravention of this Article when it results from the use of force which is no more than absolutely necessary:
(a) in defence of any person from unlawful violence;
(b) in order to effect a lawful arrest or to prevent the escape of a person lawfully detained;

(c) in action lawfully taken for the purpose of quelling a riot or insurrection.[133]

This article in turn originates in article 1 of the Universal Declaration of Human Rights (1948), which states:

All human beings are born free and equal in dignity and rights. They are endowed with reason and conscience and should act towards one another in a spirit of brotherhood.[34]

Since 1948 and the Declaration of Human Rights, which resulted from the Nuremberg Trials where the Nazis were called to answer for their crimes against humanity, this has been the benchmark for judging the morality of human behaviour. All countries which subscribe to the United Nations are judged by how closely their legal systems and practice conform to these definitions of rights. No longer is it legally permissible to argue internationally that behaviour should be judged by a different standard, although this does happen but groups such as Human Rights Watch and Amnesty International exist to monitor and criticise any such infractions. We can argue therefore there is a global morality which now overrides individual cultures, and ideologies whether religious or political. To argue therefore that human life issacrosanct in all possible cases is a distortion of the modern morality code. Much of the opposition to assisted dying emanates from a position of religious ideology that has its roots in medievalism. It is not based on the modern definition of rights but on values which belong to a religious conviction that only some unseen divinity has the right to make such decisions. This is all very well if it just concerns an

124

individual but where a person or group of people seek to impose these ideas on others, who don't share such a perspective, it is totally unacceptable. I do not see how the right to die, as defined and expressed by those of us who support assisted dying, undermines or contradicts the right to life. In fact, as Lord Underhill recognised it could in fact strengthen it by providing protection for the weak and vulnerable which doesn't in practice exist at present. At the very least, he argued this needs to be tested in court. The fact that the Divisional High Court made reference to a concept of mediaeval origin such as the sanctity of life I find highly disturbing and insulting to the majority of people in this country who are not religiously inclined. It is an extremely partisan position which is at variance, as I suggested above, with the modern world.

Chapter 8

The Mass Media

To change the law it's essential to muster a powerful publicity campaign. The media must be engaged. The emotive issue of assisted dying should not present too much of a challenge, but it is important to get the timing right and remember there will always be a loud and often emotional collection of voices against. And so it should be in a democracy. However, it is vital to be in control of this process and not at the mercy of it. I'm very pleased to say that the campaign group, Dignity in Dying, with which we have worked closely are very professional at this. Nevertheless, it is wise not to rely entirely on anyone else and to exercise one's own judgement. It has been a steep learning curve over the past year coming into contact with the media and discovering their strengths and weaknesses. A healthy wariness needs to counteract the gullibility of the novice interviewee.

Television

Traditionally television has for a long time been the premier news outlet and, although this is beginning to change with the advent of social media, it still remains a powerful agent of information dissemination, education and opinion building. Our first encounter was with BBC television news and it was quite nerve wracking anticipating what might happen. We needn't have worried, however, as the interviewer, Fergus Walsh, was extremely supportive and sympathetic. He put us at our ease immediately and I found that the previous week's practice with the media manager from the campaign group had helped more than I realised. I half expected the house to be filled with half a dozen people wielding microphones, lights and heavy cameras. As it was, there was just one cameraman who manipulated all the necessary equipment like a juggler in a circus.

There were further interviews with television crews but our overall conclusion was that the BBC were the most professional.

 To some extent, our experience with Fergus put us off our guard somewhat with the others who were more intrusive and insensitive in their approach. But as the proverb goes, *the medium is the message*. Visual stimulus is at the core of television and there is nothing better than someone dissolving into tears and displaying raw emotion to the camera. Beware that most basic, stock in trade question of the most inexperienced interviewer, '*and, how do you feel about that?* ' With its sharp intention to dig into your deepest feelings. Sometimes they were successful and both Carol and I performed like compliant seals. Later we learned to avoid this. Nor can truth and accuracy be assumed. News is biased in favour of the dramatic sound bite. Whenever I responded at length to a question, it became clear the interviewer grew inpatient until I came up with a suitable one liner that would fit the two minute exposure on prime time news. I gave them what they were looking for sometimes with the following quotes " entombed in my own body", "living like a zombie", "I don't want to die, but…."

We had initiated the campaign and therefore it was not unreasonable that I would be the main item on any of the news' reports. I was also visually effective because of the wheelchair or in my riser/recliner chair, especially with the legs up. I also use a non-invasive ventilator creating an immediate and dramatic impact. Now I understand that visual broadcasting is governed by rules regarding bias and there is a duty to present more than one side of the story. The BBC conformed to this by inviting contributors from opponents of the campaign and that was perfectly okay. The same was achieved by ITN but Channel 4 News was quite disappointing in the way it tried to do this. After a film clip of me and someone else with a terminal illness, they then shifted to the TV studio with an interviewer and someone in a wheelchair. The person in the wheelchair was not terminally ill although she was disabled. There was no one else present and the interviewer was extremely leading in the questions he posed to the campaign opponent such as *'Wouldn't this be a bad thing for disabled people?* ', '*Do you think there would be pressure on disabled people to seek an assisted death in order to avoid the expense of keeping them alive?* ' These are not exact quotes but capture the general gist of the questioning. There was an implicit acceptance that disability and being terminally ill are the same thing, which they most certainly aren't, though it is a strong contention by opponents of the campaign that they are.

Quite unexpected for both of us was that the time spent on interviewing was half that on the camera work and photography. An enormous amount of time on one occasion was consumed by getting the right angle, level and exposure for photographs. Being at the beck and call of a lens is not the romantic experience one imagines. The conclusion we drew is that being an actor or model must be a crushingly tedious occupation. Of course, today it is no longer sufficient to produce material simply for the television screen. Much of this activity was geared towards the various blogs which the news outlets now use or sell to. It is, after all, a commercial undertaking and the interviewee's interests are not necessarily the same as those of the interviewer. It may be necessary sometimes, just as we did, to say no.

The Press

Unlike television, there is no requirement for balance in the press. The people who decide how a story will be presented start with journalists. They know their readership and audience, or should do. Their efforts are then reviewed by an editor who in turn must give consideration, not only to his perspective of the readership, but also to the owner/directors of the news corporation, the law of libel and the political inclinations to which the organisation is committed. However, despite these structural biases, newspapers are often a better source of information because they can devote more time and space to an issue than broadcasting. This allows for a greater degree of analysis, often absent from television. Of course, it may well be extremely biased but the discerning reader should be aware of the nature of this i.e. whether it is a right-wing tabloid or a liberal broadsheet. The potential for nuanced argument is therefore much greater with newspapers and magazines. We found the newspaper journalists were far more relaxed in their interviewing, apart from the Daily Mail, which had a completely different agenda than the others. It wanted to show the personal angle and tried to tease out personal issues such as how we met, what we believed in and so on. In that sense, it was more personally invasive than any of the other forms of media we experienced.

Nevertheless, the press is a useful tool if used correctly. I was able to convey my message to a wide audience, emphasising those aspects I prioritised which were often omitted by the broadcasters. I was particularly anxious to counteract the notion that being terminally ill is no different than being disabled. I was very pleased therefore that the London Evening Standard asked me to write a short article for them, which I did with the help of Tom at the campaign group. Here is the finished article:

'Are you going to die? Of course you are. It's an obvious truism of being human but most of us push it to the back of our minds until and unless we are confronted with the horrors of a terrorist attack or a terrible tragedy like Grenfell Tower. Our emotional reaction is one of sympathy and compassion for the victims.

We are rarely confronted with the related existential questions of how and when we might die. Indeed few of us would want to know that. However when one is diagnosed with a terminal illness these are precisely the questions which are important.

When I was diagnosed with motor neurone disease (MND) in November 2014, my first question was the usual "how long have I got?"

I was given between six and eighteen months to live based on my symptoms and what medical statistics are available. To improve the odds, I was immediately provided with a ventilator to assist my shallow breathing and to enable me to sleep through the night. This has undoubtedly extended my life and my consultant respiratory physician has confirmed since that I would have been unlikely to survive for six months after the diagnosis without it.

Recoiling from the shock of the diagnosis, I then began to find out how I was going to die. MND is a muscle-wasting disease. It is terminal and there's no possible cure. Each individual's experience of the progression of the disease is different, but the outcome is the same: the vast majority of people with MND die from respiratory failure or infection.

The final stages are particularly horrifying. A person with MND will be encased in their body without being able to move a muscle, apart perhaps from one's eyes. The mind remains active and conscious throughout. The prospect of such an ending fills me with complete dread.

This terrible disease is the reason why I'm seeking to change the law in this country so that I can choose how I should die, by being allowed to have an assisted death.

In the High Court next week, my legal team will argue that my right to personal autonomy should be respected. At the moment I feel it's restricted by a blanket ban on assisted suicide introduced more than 50 years ago. I believe I should have the right to choose the means and timing of my death, properly supported by a doctor.

Despite considerable debate on the issue of assisted dying over the past decade, Parliament has steadfastly refused to change the law. I understand and support their concern to protect the weak and vulnerable but the blanket ban condemns me and all other terminally ill people who have six months or less to live to a degree of physical and psychological suffering which could otherwise be avoided.

There are powerful safeguards which would protect those who cannot or don't wish to exercise the option of assisted dying. There are increasing numbers of countries which now accept that this is possible, the most recent of which are Canada and several states of the US including California, Colorado and even Washington, DC.

This issue reveals an ethical dilemma: I have the right to personal autonomy and the right to life – what's often referred to as the sanctity of life. It implies a religious viewpoint harking back to traditional authority and moral paternalism. In a modern society where the rights of the individual to decide on their own lives are so sacrosanct, such a perspective is hard to sustain.

It is little wonder that the majority of people today weigh in favour of personal autonomy and support assisted dying – 78% of us according to last month's British Social Attitudes survey. Most people of faith, including leading churchmen such as Desmond Tutu and George Carey have come to support the right of mentally competent adults who are not clinically depressed to be assisted to die, but religious institutions continue to oppose it, shaped by their unreconstructed views on the sanctity of life.

The more canny religious opponents recognise that their position is no longer effective in modern discourse and so couch it amongst other nonreligious arguments.

Some disability campaign groups have become powerful opponents of assisted dying in the UK. They claim there is no distinction between being disabled and terminally ill, but have no experience of the latter.

MND has taken my ability to walk or stand, to use my hands or even raise my arms up to my head. I have used a powered wheelchair for over two years and now can only be moved by using a hoist. Like many disabled people, I require personal day-to-day support. If my current status were to remain as it is, I would be content as I continue to have some quality of life.

Unlike those who wish to deny me the right to choose my death, my disease progresses week by week, month by month and will end in my death. What I did last month, even satisfying an itch, I cannot do now. In a few months' time I'm unlikely to be able to operate my power chair. Later I will be unable to move any part of my body until finally, eventually, I die. I am terminally ill and I do not have the comfort of knowing that I will continue to live for years with my current level of immobility.

Faced with inevitable decline and an imminent death, I wish to be given the option to be helped to die. Were you in my position, wouldn't you want that too?'

12.7.17 (Draft article written for the London Evening Standard)

Social Media

Today there are so many other forms of mass communication, although that term has now been superseded by a more appropriate one that embraces so many different forms: social networking sites e.g. Facebook, blogs on Internet websites, Twitter, WhatsApp et cetera. They facilitate one-to-one communication as well as to groups or to a very wide public indeed. My own Twitter feed allows me to contact nearly 900 people directly whilst the Dignity in Dying website/Facebook

Page extends to a readership of over 300,000. And when a message goes 'viral 'it means that it is transported piggyback style from platform to platform and in that way can become global and reach millions. Because of this, and its popularity with a new potential readership, that would not otherwise be reached via their more traditional channels, both broadcasters and press have their own websites and blogs. Some people have their own blogs but I am content with Twitter as I would find it too physically demanding to create and maintain my own. Nonetheless, I have had the opportunity of contributing to blogs, the first of which was on the Dignity in Dying website that is still there and one for Sky News, May 2018 regarding the next step of the legal fight in the Appeals Court, as follows:

'Imagine you have motor neurone disease – an incurable, terminal disease that will kill you, but not before it causes progressive deterioration of the muscles throughout your body. You have three choices about how to die.

The first one involves removing a breathing aid, which is used for 22 hours a day, and will result in breathlessness and suffocation that can only be relieved by medication. Unfortunately, the medication will cause a state of drowsy semi-consciousness until death occurs. This experience may last for a few hours or a few days; no one knows and no one can say how much that will alleviate the sensation of fighting for breath.

The second choice is to wait until the breathing aid is used all the time, so that when removed death will come more swiftly. However, the drawback here is that the body will by then have become virtually immobile. What must it be like to lie there unable to move one's head from side to side, to be able to move only one's eyes. I have some premonition of that now, when I don't even have the strength to get my arms and hands from beneath the sheet and single blanket which I use at night. It takes a great deal of self-control not to panic.

Finally, there is the choice, if the law is changed, to permit assisted dying in this country. In this case you could, if terminally ill and mentally sound, choose the right moment to say goodbye to the ones you love, request life-ending medication, perhaps in liquid form for you to suck through a straw, and wait a few minutes to fall into a coma followed by the merciful release of death.

The importance of the above is to be able to imagine what might happen if you were in our position; to empathise with me and thousands of others in like circumstances. Think about it now, close your eyes, feel your way into each scenario. What would you choose?

Unfortunately, neither you nor I have that third choice at the moment. Our choices are severely restricted to an end-of-life experience which may well involve some degree of suffering, the depth of which is unknown.

I was diagnosed with motor neurone disease in November 2014. I have the classic form, which is known as amyotrophic lateral sclerosis (ALS). The life expectation for ALS is 2 to 5 years from the date of diagnosis. However, I know that my symptoms began at least two years before this date when I

started losing weight, felt a pain in my lower back and increasingly began to have difficulty walking.

I now can no longer walk at all and have to be hoisted from bed to chair, as well as experiencing increasing difficulty with breathing and having to wear my ventilator for 22 hours a day. This is a far cry from the life I led before my diagnosis – one in which my wife Carol, our children and I walked every inch of the Shropshire Hills around our home and regularly went on cycling, skiing and climbing trips across the UK and abroad.

When I was diagnosed, the shock was overwhelming. For Carol and I, it signalled the end of all our plans for the future (I had just retired two months before). We had a holiday in China planned for the following year and we were looking forward to visiting those parts of the world which we had not done such as the USA and Australasia.

All of this was in tatters. I felt like a condemned man awaiting execution on a date yet to be determined. I became aware of how agonising it must be to be someone on death row for years and years not knowing when the order will come.

As my condition has continued to deteriorate and I have become more aware of what will happen, I have become increasingly focused on end-of-life concerns and what options are (or aren't) available to me. Absurdly, the only way terminally ill people can extend our end-of-life choices is, where it is practicable, to take our own life alone at home, or rely on a loved one to help us at the end by accompanying us, if we have the means, to travel to Switzerland. One could attempt to obtain medication illegally over the Internet, but without the guarantee of knowing whether it will work or whether it will be without agonising pain.

I dread the first two choices. Due to the deterioration caused by my illness, I am now quadriplegic and therefore my options for ending my life without undue suffering are limited. Once in my power wheelchair, I may just have sufficient mobility in my right hand to plunge off a path into a fast flowing river, or off the side of a railway platform into an oncoming train. Although these options are real, I cannot accept them, because they would hurt other people too much.

The third option, far from hurting others, would give me the opportunity, in my final months, to decide when the time is right for me to go and to leave this world swiftly and with dignity. Faced with the same choices, what would you choose?'

28 February 2018 (Draft written for Sky News)

The example given above has of course been edited but this is not always the case and it is possible to receive negative as well as positive messages via social media. I have been fortunate to date with my Twitter feed because I have received very few negative or bizarre comments, although there have been one or two. For example, **'if you want to go kill yourself, it is easy, so why don't you do so '.** The strangest comment I received was from someone claiming to be a doctor in the USA who said there was a cure for MND and that I should contact him forthwith for details. Needless to say, I didn't follow this idiotic comment up and if he was a medical doctor it would be a highly irresponsible claim to make. On a more positive vote, I have received personal messages of support from ex-students and made contact with some old friends from secondary school days that I had lost touch with.

Chapter 9

Advanced Directive to Refuse Treatment (ADRT)

To be in charge when one takes one's final breath is what my campaign is all about. And there is a way to do this - make out an Advanced Directive to Refuse Treatment. By this means people can decide such things as where they would wish to die, who they would like present, whether or not they would like all assistance available to prevent death. It is surprising that many of us don't give sufficient thought to our final days though there are now campaigns encouraging people to do so.

Carol and I had considered it a few years ago when Carol's mother died. The impersonal, even cold way in which she ended her life in hospital moved us to think deeply about our own demise. My own mother died many years ago and I remember seeing her for the last three weeks in hospital, which she feared and hated, being treated like a piece of meat until it has passed its sell by date and needs throwing out. I was not aware at the time, nor were any other members of the family, about the possibilities of ADRT, or what was becoming called in some places 'a Living Will'. But at the time of Betty's death, Carol's mother, there was information about it on the Internet, which is where we first completed our 'Living Wills'. We asked two friends to sign as witnesses but I don't know how valid they would have been. Following my diagnosis with MND, the first thing that the Palliative Care Consultant suggested was the advisability of drawing up and ADRT that she would help us with. She provided us with an electronic pro forma and we transferred our first earlier attempts to that. When we discussed it with her we were able to go into a lot more depth and consider issues that we hadn't done before because I wasn't suffering from MND. This was an invaluable exercise and enabled us to really think about what should happen at the end and be ready for any unforeseen events. We then obtained two friends' signatures as witnesses and we lodged a copy with our solicitors, which didn't cost us anything. We also made sure that other members of the medical health support team were provided with copies, especially our GP.

One is not bound by the ADRT even at the time of death and its provisions could be rescinded by oneself or one's nominee, usually a spouse, who has been identified as having right of attorney. However, what it does do is to help prepare for the final days very effectively. It is not a substitute for assisted dying which, if it were to become law, could be specified as well. It is understandable why people do not give much thought to these matters but when death or dying becomes imminent it is a great relief to one's nearest and dearest to have something to guide them to comply with the dying person's wishes.

I have selected a few key passages for information from my current ADRT to show the sorts of things that can be covered. Bear in mind, this could change and it is advisable to review it regularly:

My Advanced Decision to Refuse Treatment

1: What is this document for?

This document has been completed by me or with my authorisation. It states in advance any treatments I do not want in the future, under specific circumstances. This form replaces any previous ADRT that I have made.

It should only be used if I can no longer refuse or consent to treatment because I have become unable to make or communicate (by any means of communication) decisions about my healthcare.

By completing this document, I understand it is still my right to receive basic care, support and comfort.

Advice to anyone reading my ADRT:

Before any actions are taken, please do not assume I have lost capacity to make decisions or to communicate. I may need help time to communicate.

If I have lost capacity, please check the validity and applicability of this ADRT. If it is valid and applicable, please ensure that you act on it, as it is a legal document.

Please help to share this information with relevant colleagues involved in my treatment and care, who need to know about this.

Please also check if I have made any other statements about my preferences or wishes that might be relevant to my advance decisions.

2: My condition

In relation to my health problems, I have been diagnosed with the following:	
Motor neurone disease (MND), a life-shortening condition that has no cure.	
This affects me in the following ways:	
I am becoming progressively weaker. This condition causes great problems with	

daily activities including breathing and mobility.	
I have talked about my feelings with my family. This is the right time for me to make my advance decisions about my future care and treatment	as I am having increasing as I difficulties with my breathing.
I know MND will shorten my life and I wish to make choices about what will happen with my future care and treatment at end of life.	
My advance decisions in this ADRT state any treatments I wish to refuse or withdraw if they are no longer working and have become a burden	even if this means my life is at risk.

3: My advance decisions

The following instructions state which treatments I wish to refuse and the precise circumstances in which each action will apply.

Unless stated otherwise below, I confirm that the following decisions to refuse treatment are to apply '**even if my life is at risk**' (please tick this box if you agree with this statement):	
I wish to refuse the following specific treatments:	In these circumstances:
Cardio-pulmonary resuscitation (re-starting my heart and breathing)	I wish to refuse cardio-pulmonary resuscitation in the event that I have a cardiac or respiratory arrest due to the impact of motor neurone disease or any related condition, such

	as a severe chest infection.
Invasive ventilation (where a machine breathes for you following a tracheostomy)	I wish to receive non-invasive ventilatory support to manage my symptoms but I wish to refuse invasive ventilation via tracheostomy.
Non - invasive ventilation (where a machine helps to support your own breathing through a mask)	I wish to have non-invasive ventilation withdrawn if despite simple attempts to position me, clear my airway and remove secretions, I can no longer breathe by

	myself without the help of the machine.
Artificial feeding via gastrostomy tube (PEG/RIG)	When my Motor Neurone Disease has deteriorated to the point that I cannot swallow sufficiently to meet my nutritional requirements, I do not wish to receive artificial nutrition via a gastrostomy tube
Antibiotics (to treat a severe, life threatening chest infection)	I wish to refuse antibiotics in the event that I have a severe chest infection that may threaten my life.

There is a view that refusal to accept treatment is akin to assisted dying because it results in the same end, death. In both cases, medical professionals would be participants in some way because their natural and professional duty is to prevent death at all events. However, the ADRT makes it very clear that the patient's wishes must be adhered to and it is recognised in law that the decision will have been made when he or she was mentally competent, although rather interestingly there is no requirement to prove this at the time it is drawn up. Furthermore, when the patient is in the final few hours of dying and is very likely to be semi or even unconscious, it is arguable that they are far from being in a state of mental competence. Still the law requires that the patient's autonomy is respected according to what is written down and signed by witnesses, unless of course the patient has indicated at the last moment that he or she has changed her mind and wishes to be for example resuscitated. In my view the completion of an ADRT is a proactive action which is no different from assisted dying because the patient still has to perform the final act him/herself and is not passive. Why is it regarded as being different? Medical professionals opposed would claim they are being asked to participate actively in bringing about the death of a patient, which is against their ethics, but in fact they are not completing the final act. As the medical profession in this country controls access to the drugs necessary to end one's life, it is inevitable that they are involved but really they are merely gatekeepers and it is the power of their profession which puts them in that position. If this were changed, as it is in other countries e.g. Peru, they wouldn't be involved at all. Philosophically this whole debate effectively revolves around whose autonomy is to be respected, the patient's or the doctor's?

There is another difference between assisted dying and the ADRT. This relates to the choice of time of death. In the latter, one waits for the effects of the illness or condition to take its course, whilst with the former one decides when to the very hour and minute. Assisted dying has the added advantage that it removes the likelihood of any potential suffering which may occur whilst waiting for an infection to carry one-off. So, whilst the ADRT provides a certain degree of control over how one can end one's life, it is limited.

Chapter 10

Beginning of the Journey?

W ho can say when anything truly begins and ends? Western philosophy predisposes us to think in a linear way, of cause and effect, of origins and endings but Eastern philosophy does not. Buddhists and Taoists think of circular processes where there cannot be such a simple explanation of how the cosmos works. Even time itself, Einstein has told us, is relative and a human construct. When we know so little about Motor Neurone Disease, it is not fanciful to speculate on where its origins may lie in an individual human being.

I was born in 1949 in a Blackburn nursing home to Jennifer and Douglas Conway. They were quite typical in some ways of their generation but unlike it in others. They didn't meet until 1947 and had a quite different experience of wartime Britain. What they had in common were their working class origins in north-east Lancashire and an appetite for adventure. My father was a bright lad and received prizes for reading and geography at the Boys' Central School in Blackburn. He left school at the age of 15 years to take an apprenticeship as a printer at the Lancashire Evening Telegraph. As was often the way at that time, when he reached 16 years of age and the employer had to pay for his health insurance, he was made redundant. He picked from amongst what little work was available at the time, which was in a greengrocer's shop in town. War was looming and he couldn't wait to become 18 years old when he could enlist as a volunteer. This was in 1940 and he was duly sent to Portsmouth to train as a Royal Marine, which he remained until 1945. His duties were largely policing and escorting convoys but he travelled from North Africa to Sicily, Italy, France and Germany. When he left the Navy he became a fireman with Blackburn Fire Service. He didn't meet my mother until the immediate years following the war at one of the many dance halls that proliferated at the time for the young people who had survived the wartime ordeal and were letting their hair down and celebrating life with great enthusiasm.

My mother had experienced an easy and comfortable war, if that is not an oxymoron. She was one of four girls brought up in Accrington in a mixed faith family, which today would signify something quite different but then it referred to the fact her father was of Irish extraction and Roman Catholic, whilst her mother was a staunch Anglican. In those days, the Roman Catholic Church held considerable sway over its congregation and the condition for blessing the union was that the first two children born were to be baptised into the Roman Catholic Church and the last two, at my grandmother's insistence, be raised as Anglicans.

My mother was a great beauty, inveterate gossip and extremely sociable. In those days of high unemployment, she was fortunate to obtain work as an usherette in one of the local cinemas. It was during this period that this young, self-consciously confident 18 year old working class lass with the sharp features of an Irish beauty, was noticed by a well-to-do 36-year-old male. Jack was a successful chemist with ICI and certainly had an eye for the ladies. He whisked her off her feet and they were married in 1938. For my mother, this was a new beginning as she holidayed in Switzerland, climbed the Jung Frau, went skiing and got used to feasting at tables on dishes she had never heard of before. Ignoring the war as much as was possible, they were wealthy enough to have a large house built on the western outskirts of Blackburn. Jack's job was considered essential to the war effort so he had permission to run a car throughout the war years frequently travelling into Manchester for work. Everything must have seemed rather wonderful at first for my mother, but for reasons not known to me, she suspected he was having an affair and this turned out to be the case. I'm not sure exactly when this was, but at the end of the war they agreed to annul the marriage. She extracted from him, and I don't think that's too strong a word to use, a house purchased outright in a plush suburb of Blackburn, a car and a £200 a year annuity, which in those days was sufficient for her to live on without working. Jack was evidently made to pay heavily for his wartime dalliances. From all accounts, she and her girlfriends had a whale of a time until they began to meet more permanent partners, pairing off and finally marrying, as my mother and father did.

My father had a relatively good job immediately after he was demobbed as a fireman and when they married they were able to purchase their own home. They were clearly better off than most people at that time and this would be, of course, as a consequence of my mother's marriage settlement. Whether that gave her more clout than was normal at that time in the relationship, I can't be sure. On the one hand, my father was quite phlegmatic and even-tempered, whilst my mother, rather like myself, was strong-willed and prone to flaring up at the slightest provocation. On the other hand, my father's natural intelligence probably gave him the upper hand, but I think for most of the time they gelled well and operated as an equal partnership. My father didn't stay in the fire service for long, obtaining employment as a dental salesman, which meant he was supplied with a car for his work. I suspect my mother was behind this because she was now quite a snob and looked down on others she considered inferior. At some stage, the momentous decision was taken to emigrate to New Zealand. This was prior to the £10 assisted passages scheme which came in by 1950. Who was responsible for this move I can only guess at but I know my father was something of a nomad by temperament, probably as a result of his wartime experiences, although I don't think this would have been sufficient to separate my mother from her sisters and family to whom she was close. I think the catalyst was the death of their firstborn son, the 'baby Douglas ', who died before I was born of an infection he picked up in hospital after being admitted for swallowing some unknown berries. I know that it affected them both very deeply, but I believe my father was the more damaged by it than my mother because for the rest of his life, I discovered later, he took a course of antidepressants. A fresh start in a new land is often a good way of leaving traumatic events behind.

So, like Magellan hundreds of years before, I circumnavigated half the globe via the Panama Canal on a six weeks passage to New Zealand. I was oblivious to this remarkable journey being at the tender age of nine months. We weren't to return for more than five years, when I was almost 6 years old, complete with a baby sister, Beverley, and a Kiwi accent. On the journey home, from Sydney, Australia, via Ceylon and the Suez Canal, I almost died from some mysterious virus. No one else on board seems to have been affected so it must not have been infectious. What was it and did it leave me to flareup nearly 60 years later? As far as I can remember, it was a happy time in New Zealand where I grew from a baby to a toddler and then a little boy. My parents seemed happy and content. We had bought a house in a suburb of Wellington called Cara Cara. The days seemed sunny and endless, broken only by the odd earthquake. I have a powerful memory of one occasion when my bed moved from one side of the room to the other. There was sand and dirt to dig in, butterflies to chase, a horse to be given rides on with Mary, a young female friend of the family, and a doting mother who was always there. The only blight on this paradise was my little sister, whom I tried to get rid of by filling her pram with sand while she was still in it. Another lingering image is of my mother's panic when I was bitten by something called a ' wetter ', which I think is a biting spider or beetle unique to New Zealand. So why did we have to leave and return to the damp, cold dreariness of the UK? Was it because we ran out of money, was it because of Mary, or was it because of the earthquakes? The official reason was that my mother was homesick and missing her family dreadfully. Well, perhaps this was so but I think it must have been a dreadful wrench for my father to leave his island paradise. I believe he was perfectly at home there. It's certainly true that in those days migrating to the other side of the world was like moving to the moon. Communications were difficult, by letter only, which took weeks to arrive and there was little hope or prospect of seeing old friends and relatives ever again. It was akin to a death sentence but I do wonder why they returned, at their own expense, when they must have known all this beforehand.

Returning to the grim industrial landscapes of the North must have been deeply depressing for my father. For a time, we lived with my father's mother for nearly a year in Blackburn. Or, I should say, my father did because after a few months my volatile mother had seriously fallen out with her mother-in-law and trounced off with her two children back to her own in Accrington. For six months, until the new house we were waiting for to be built was completed, my sister and I slept head to toe with our cousins on my mother's side. When we finally moved in to the little, compact bungalow on the outskirts of Blackburn, my father and mother were reconciled. Frequent trips to Accrington, nevertheless, continued and we tried as best we could to get used to the wet, gloomy atmosphere of a northern industrial town. We must still have had money because that year we holidayed for two weeks in a hotel on full board in Falmouth, Cornwall, overlooking the main beach. The Mediterranean blue like sky combined with the lazy heat of an Indian summer was enough to stimulate my father's wanderlust again. None of us wanted to return home.

When we did, my father continually talked about how marvellous Falmouth had been and then, before I had got used to my new primary school, plans were afoot for us to move again. I vividly recall the steam-train en route to our new destination. It was a very long day and I remember sleeping in the luggage rack until we arrived in Truro, the capital of our newly discovered Shangri-La. The following day, a taxi took us to a caravan site on the outskirts of Falmouth. It was a tiny caravan on a holiday site where we stayed just long enough for my parents to find somewhere more permanent for us to live.

In the end, we spent two harmonious years living in a nearby residential Park, where the people were friendly and helpful. How on earth my mother put up with all this, I don't know? We were poor but very happy. The genuine community that surrounded us compensated for the lack of material goods. The caravan, like most of them then, was not very big. There was a small galley kitchen, a broom cupboard which housed the all-important metal pail for the overnight slops, a living room with a pull down table, which also converted into a double bed for my parents, and a tiny little bedroom with two ship's bunks for my sister and I. There was no electricity and we relied totally on camping gas. We had no television, only a single battery radio. Despite these apparent privations, it was one of the happiest times of my life. There is nothing to equal the soft glow from a gas mantle lighting up the dusk and the gentle whispering hiss from the supply pipes. My father found what work he could, but there was little to be had as this was now a depressed area economically and did not benefit from any post-war economic boom as did the rest of the country. The main economy around Falmouth had been international shipping in the days well before containers and everything had to be loaded on and off by hand and trolley. For six months of the year, my father became a docker or a welder's mate working in the dangerous and confined spaces of old transatlantic ships, which would soon be scrapped. Roads in and out of the south-west for many decades to come were incapable of coping with the transit requirements of a booming economy and therefore ports closer to London in the south-east were used in place of Falmouth, which for centuries had been a major harbour for Britain's international trade.

Unfortunately, this happy time would not last. My grandfather back in Blackburn had become seriously ill with bowel cancer. In those days there were no hospices and families were expected to look after their own. As the younger of two brothers without a steady job, my father was duty-bound to go home to support his mother and look after his father in his final days. He seemed to be away for weeks but eventually the inevitable happened and my grandfather died a painful death. A further momentous move was just around the corner for the family. My mother and father had been saving hard for a small deposit on a newly built house that we had all been to see and were quite excited about, but now these hopes were dashed because my father was expected to return home to support his mother. His elder brother had a good civil service job in Edinburgh and thus it was not considered appropriate by any of the family for him to make the sacrifice that my father had to. As you can imagine, my mother was once again furious but she did not show much of it to us children. This time, when we returned to Blackburn, we had fewer resources and even less money. Fortunately, we were returning to a Labour constituency which had provided well for the housing needs of its population and so we were able to apply successfully for a newly built council house not too far away from the centre of town. For the first year, I had to continue travelling on two buses from my new home to my old primary school, St Gabriel's, which was in a district called Rowe Lee, where we had stayed with my grandma for a year after returning from Cornwall. When I eventually transferred to the secondary school, it was a relief to only have to catch one bus into town followed by a 20 minute walk.

My education had clearly suffered whilst I was in Cornwall as I was struggling with maths, though my English was good. However, it meant I failed the 11+ and could not hope to attend the prestigious Blackburn Grammar school. Instead, I was allocated a place at St Peter's C of E school in an old part of the town, next to a rather stinking glue making factory and a mile away from its girls' counterpart, St Hilda's, which my sister attended. The two schools often collaborated in joint projects such as pageants and religious services. In 1966, to my great joy and pleasure the two combined into one overall co-educational comprehensive school, St Wilfred's.

For whatever reason, possibly on the basis of my 11+ marks, I was allocated to the A stream. There were four streams, A - D. Only the A and B streams were entered for exams of any kind and only the A stream were entered for GCE O-levels. St Peter's could be a rough school with some rather scary types who were reputed to stick new boys' heads down lavatories, but in reality there was not much of this and it was always possible to outrun the bullies. I soon made some good friends, some of whom I have re-established contact with recently. It was not a grammar school and the teaching was of mixed quality, though there were some very dedicated and able teachers. In particular, I recall four teachers who were very generous with their time with those of us who wanted to learn and sympathetic to our position as working-class boys, who had just failed the 11+ exam. There was Mr Sharples, who was in charge of physical education within the school and, as I proved to be a considerable athlete all-rounder as well as gymnast, provided a lot of support to me personally. For four nights a week after school, he and his staff organised many training programmes, which meant the school was a leading one in the town for cross-country, athletics and football. Then there was Mr McLean, who joined the school when I was in the third year. His strictly run classes in mathematics, enabled the scales to fall from my eyes so that instead of receiving 3% in the end of year exams, I started to achieve pass level grades. I began to enjoy geometry and even algebra. By the time I took GCE O-level I was competent enough to receive a credit grade.

 Finally, there were two special teachers there who were to have a profound influence on my personal development. Henry Dickinson, was a youngish 30 something's teacher of religious studies who joined the school when I was in my second year. He was an ex-monk but an excellent teacher who stimulated discussion and free debate. He encouraged the pupils to think for themselves and listened to their concerns sympathetically. He was dedicated to the Anglican church and played an important part in the life of the local church, St Peter's. From the third year onwards, he also organised music trips to the Halle Orchestra in Manchester or Bolton where there were often string quartet recitals. It was because of Henry and these trips that I acquired an appreciation of classical music. Then there was Roy Williams, who was the vicar of St Peter's and school chaplain. He was a very bright individual

158

who had won a scholarship to Oxford to read classics, in which he excelled obtaining a First. This was all the more remarkable as he came from a very poor family in a depressed area of Manchester. This would explain his politics, as he was, as I became, a dedicated socialist and member of the Labour Party. From Henry and Roy I received a supplementary education, along with two or three of my friends who they deemed equally able to benefit from more than the secondary modern education we were receiving at school. I must be one of the few 11+ failures who also failed O-level Latin and Greek, but I thoroughly enjoyed the instruction and the broader historical horizons that this study entailed. It was because of these two extraordinary individuals that I set my sights on University, which would definitely not have happened had it been left entirely to my parents, for whom that was a land too far, even in the 60s. Their ambitions for me at that time were to become a PE teacher. Instead I was motivated to apply for religious studies and philosophy, as well as history and economics at various Northern universities with a view to obtaining a degree followed by entry into the seminary to train as an Anglican priest.

Before I even entered University, my faith was undergoing a seismic transformation. In hindsight, I explain it as undertaking a personal Reformation. I was pretty arrogant at that time, though I don't really know why since my intelligence did not warrant it and still doesn't. It was probably part of the Angry Young Man syndrome or, to put it another way, the relatively intelligent working class lad with a chip on his shoulder. It's possible that I merely reflected the Zeitgeist of the period. The mid-to-late 60s was a time when youth challenged traditional authority in the hope of creating a better society. That itself was an arrogant perspective because the previous generation had been born of war and had sacrificed everything to create a free and independent society for future generations. Talk about ungrateful children and you talk about the 60s generation. Affluent beyond measure and hedonistic beyond sense. Of course, at the time, we were breaking new ground and going well beyond, or so we thought, any that had gone before. The subsequent decade of the 70s revealed how empty, selfish and nihilistic we had become. I was hardly Martin Luther but I had the audacity to query the traditional hierarchy and form of worship of the Anglican church. Why, I asked, was it only in churches that worship should take place? Why were intermediaries such as priests and bishops needed to communicate with God? Roy tried to make me see into the depths of that ancient tradition and how important it was to maintain it. But whatever explanations he provided, they didn't seem to be sufficient. When I arrived at Lancaster University, I was introduced in the philosophy course to Ludwig Feuerbach, whose '*On Religion* 'had profoundly influenced Karl Marx. It was a continuation of Hegel's work in which he stood the prevailing order on its head arguing that rather than God having created Man, it was the other way round - Man had created God. The idea that the divine and the Godhead was a projection of men's minds stunned me. I could not shake the fundamental truth of it. It was as if I had been lied to since birth, like the story of Father Christmas, but now the scales fell from my eyes and I saw clearly for the first time. My increasing knowledge of Marxism strengthened this perspective. The Marxian concept of ideology as a social construct to maintain the class structure and the denunciation of religion as nothing but 'the opiate of the people ' made total sense to me. It was no wonder therefore that I dropped

160

religious studies for economics, which didn't help me settling in during this first year. I was also very much aware of being working class whilst many of my university peers were from middle-class and even public school backgrounds. Little wonder, therefore, that I began to return home each weekend to see my girlfriend and the family but this made it more difficult to settle in and accept separation from home. Consequently, I did not return after the first term to the great disappointment of Henry and even my parents. For a time, I didn't know what to do but my father, quite rightly, said I would have to obtain work and in the meantime claim benefits from Social Security. What a rude awakening it was for me and an experience at the Dole Office, where I learned how society treated the less well off by keeping them waiting many hours, regarding them as if they were nothing more than scroungers. Unlike today, however, there was a lot of work available and someone like me with A-levels was in high demand in the financial services sector.

I found a job as an insurance trainee in Bolton where I stayed for the next four years. During that time I married my first wife, Pauline, and had my first child - a lovely little girl, Ashley. Our first place was a rented apartment over a shop on the edge of a council estate on the border between Blackburn and Darwin. There were two bedrooms, a small living room, bathroom and a reasonably sized kitchen. It was clean and free of infestation. The only problem was its location, which meant there was quite a walk to a bus stop and the centre of town. Nevertheless, it served us well for 18 months until we moved in with a friend in a sort of commune arrangement. That didn't quite work out. Idealistic alternative lifestyles were all the rage at that time, but it didn't take long for reality to set in and we began to hanker after our own private space, so in less than six months we had moved out and bought a terraced house in the area coincidentally that my parents had first lived, Little Harwood. By this time, however, the area was experiencing something of an economic decline and it wouldn't be long before immigrants from Southeast Asia, principally Pakistan, began to buy properties nearby.

I was a local Labour councillor by then representing a ward adjacent to where I lived, occupied at that time 50-50 by newcomers and indigenous born and bred Blackburnians. It was the repository of the first wave of Pakistani immigrants who came, attracted by the prospect of work in the surrounding cotton mills. For many of the locals, most of whom were retired or too poor to move anywhere else, it was a considerable shock and relations were difficult to establish between the two communities. I was caught in the middle. Sympathetic, on the one hand, to the plight of the immigrants, but also sensitive to the feelings of the local residents, on the other. There was nothing by way of interracial meetings and when the local Labour Council was perceived as granting special privileges to the incomers, widespread resentment grew towards the Labour Party. Issues about the opening up of cemeteries at week-end to accommodate the Islamic requirement to bury the dead as soon as possible, the granting of butchery licences to dubious premises where halal meat could be prepared and the proliferation of unclean rubbish in backyards from illegal slaughtering practices, became significant areas of conflict. It also seemed to be that the local Labour Party/Ruling Council used these areas as bargaining ploys to obtain the Muslim vote, which was marshalled according to ethnic group rather than individual choice. The

162

Party could rely on a 100% turnout from them. This was far from democratic and broke all the rules of balloting when wives and adult children were told who to vote for, or, more often than not, their votes were collected by elders of the community, abusing the postal balloting system for chronically sick and elderly people. This was a dangerous precedent which would be exploited increasingly over the next decades with the local Labour Party in thrall to the local Muslim community to whom it granted planning permission for the building of many mosques and madrases that now characterise certain parts of the town.

It was at this time that Blackburn, rather unsurprisingly, became a centre for the growth of the British National Party a more vigorous, new offshoot of the National Front. There was at least one BNP councillor elected during that time and marches and counter marches proliferated. Residential areas were sharply racially delineated and it was impossible for Muslims to buy property or live in peace in some neighbourhoods of the town. They would be forced out by a series of harassing techniques such as bricks through the window, shouting abuse at the family whenever they stepped out into the street or in the worst cases, arson attacks by shoving burning rags through the letterboxes. It was not all one-way. A few years later my own nephew was attacked by a group of Muslim youths and severely beaten walking on his way home from town. Today, Blackburn cannot be described as anything else than a segregated and divided community. When I reflect back to that time I do so with shame, feeling that I ought to have had more insight and ability to try to prevent this, in however small a way.

After three years in the insurance business, despite success in the professional exams, I knew it was not the future for me. My wife Pauline was working, Ashley went to the excellent local nursery school and obtaining a university place secured a grant which one could live on. I therefore returned to higher education when I enrolled on a Sociology Degree course at what was then Preston Polytechnic, licensed by the University of London to offer degrees. It was to be my way out of Blackburn and the beginnings of a whole new phase in my life.

I was once asked by a psychologist who was carrying outa.m.ini Mental Examination on me, whether I felt guilty about anything I had done. I was not quite sure what he was getting at because I would defy anyone not to feel guilty about something or some part of their past life. It may be just a straightforward question probing the degree of psychosis which we all possess to some extent, but I could not help reflecting later whether it signified something else. If there is a deeply buried secret or guilt in one, could that grow like a metaphorical cancer and perhaps act as a catalyst for some physical malfunctioning of one's physiology? Who knows? But if it does, then this was a time in my life that may have produced it. I felt that whilst I had remained in Blackburn, many of my friends having left, shot the nest, undertaking courses in teacher training colleges or degrees at university. Re-entering higher education at the age of 22 years, I felt I was a young 18 year old again able to experiment with life as though I didn't have family responsibilities. The upshot was that when I successfully completed my course and a further one, allowing me to secure a job in further education as a lecturer, this became the parting of the ways for Pauline and me. What I hadn't reckoned on, however, was the strength of my emotions for my daughter for whom I wished to continue to take responsibility and be a part of her life. In the end, my wife and daughter ended up living in Smethwick in Birmingham for a while, whilst I obtained a house in the new town of Telford which went along with my job. It soon became clear that I could not sustain travelling to and fro to see my daughter for long and as it transpired, the feelings between Pauline and I were not totally dead. Not only had I experienced a huge feeling of loss i.e. my family, but also one of terrific guilt for what I had brought about. Consequently, I threw out the critical sociological theory of the family and re-embraced that institution as one of the most basic essentials for mental health and happiness in life.

Chapter 11

Early Adult Life

Before I left Blackburn in 1976 to settle in Telford, the period from 1970 was a curiously unsettling one. I had embarked on the first steps of adult hood by marrying at 20 years of age, having a child and living in a home of my own. I wasn't clear what the future would be for both me and my family but I threw myself into various activities and interests with all the energy that a healthy young man possesses. Family life was a novelty that unfolded before me.

I applied myself to my professional studies in insurance with gusto and began to make some progress at work after my first year training. I was not attracted at all to the selling side of insurance, so I think any long-term career prospects would have been limited, but I found insurance law and the technical side of fire insurance much more attractive. Eventually, I became a fire insurance surveyor and underwriter, at branch level. I was also appointed as deputy in the fire insurance department in the Bolton branch of the Provincial Insurance company. I suppose I have always been a bit of a nerd because I enjoyed the detail required in drawing up plans for a fire survey, which required visiting the premises and talking to customers. An equally tricky part of the job was to assess risk and be able to quote a rate for it which would not bankrupt the company by being too low or too great a fire risk. My mentor at this time was the head of the fire department at the branch, Tony, who was Oxford educated and an excellent teacher. He was also widely knowledgeable, sensitive and tolerant. We strayed well beyond the boundaries of insurance matters in some of our discussions, which were often either about politics or religion in which he was much better educated than I. With a degree in PPE you might have expected him to be condescending and patronising but he wasn't and I appreciated his company, erudition and his mind immensely.

I very much enjoyed my time working in Bolton, which had an excellent Smith's bookshop in the centre, close to the branch office where I worked. I bought quite a few classics at that time and had the vague notion of building a library, which ultimately I have and some of those early purchases remain a part of it. On warm sunny days, I would spend a pleasurable lunch hour on a bench in a churchyard reading Thomas Hardy or a Shakespeare play. One of my favourites at this time was Hardy's *Jude the Obscure* with whom I could readily identify. I too felt shut outside the walls of academia and it wouldn't be long before I realised I had to return there.

167

During this time my political activities increased. I had first started out with the Labour Party as a runner in the 1964 General Election and again in 1966. In 1970, a disappointing defeat for the Labour Party nationally, I was put in charge of a ward with the responsibility of getting the vote out. This was in the fiefdom of the red Baroness, Barbara Castle, who maintained a healthy majority for 30 years. It was then I first met the redoubtable MP herself who was doing the rounds. Shortly after, when I had reached my 21st birthday, I was prevailed upon to contest St Luke's ward as a county borough councillor in the forthcoming elections. It was almost a foregone conclusion that I would win this as the numbers of Muslims in the area had continued to grow. I had also completed a minor apprenticeship by standing in a predominantly Tory ward where, of course, I didn't win. Nonetheless I had shown willing, knocked on a few doors, posted a few leaflets and even turned up at the count where I gave some vacuous speech. It was enough to show the local worthies that I was serious. I now had a Ward of my own to run and I set about it enthusiastically by rearranging the front room of the little Victorian terraced house we lived in at the time so it had a desk, telephone and filing cabinet. I was soon quite busy dealing with constituency queries, attending council meetings, party meetings, group meetings, ward meetings et cetera. There was no end to meetings and I spent 4/5 evenings during the week attending them.

One of the most contentious issues I remember from this time was when the Tory Government of Ted Heath introduced a Housing Bill that was going to force local authorities to raise council rents. This was the first of the post-war Tory

168

Governments which aimed to remove the powers of local government, ostensibly for the reasons of controlling the economy, but it was really about preventing Labour-controlled authorities from protecting their constituents from indirect Tory tax rises. I along with other left-wing Labour councillors were prepared to oppose this move by refusing to support the increase in rents required. We saw it as nothing less than class warfare. However, the leader of the Labour group, the later ennobled Lord Tom Taylor, and other senior Labour Council members, tried to impose a three line whip requiring us to implement the Act in full. They argued with the full support of council officers, that we had no choice but to do this or powers would be taken away from the Council and rents would be increased anyway. They were not up for a fight but they were with their own colleagues! The Government had also warned all councillors throughout the UK, who refused to increase their housing rents, would be surcharged. This meant that any councillor voting against the Act would be liable personally for any loss of income to the Local Authority and would have their financial assets seized to the amount of the costs and loss of putative rent incurred. The issue brought out divisions within the party locally and in the group. It became very emotional and I suppose it was a precursor to the rise of Militant Tendency a few years later. The vote came to full Council and I and the other rebels voted against it. Each of us was then disciplined by being summoned before the leader of the group, his deputy and chair of the local party demanding to know whether we were likely to repeat this action and that if so we would be expelled from the party. I think we all gave assurances that we would not repeat the action but I knew that if it were to happen again I would vote in exactly the same way. That was not the end of the matter. A few months later, I and the other rebels were summoned before the Local Government Ombudsman, who had been approached by local Tories arguing that we should be prosecuted for trying to prevent the collection of monies due to the Council from the increased rents. It was an absurd charade because the money had already been collected and there were no losses. Nevertheless all the rebels, including me, were issued with a *certificate of default* which would record our dereliction of duty as a representative of the people remaining potentially operative in perpetuity. At the time, I transferred what few assets I and my wife owned into my wife's name alone as a precaution. I still have that certificate but I must confess it doesn't give me sleepless nights.

One of the few memorable occasions that I recall with pleasure from this political phase of my life was when I met the Prime Minister, Harold Wilson. He had been invited to his fellow Cabinet Minister's constituency to celebrate something or other that I can't remember now. A shindig was organised for all the faithful in the grandiose King George's Hall in the centre of Blackburn, where both Harold and Barbara addressed the local party. After the speeches, I remember walking away from the main bar with two drinks in my hands and coming across a rather short, squat figure in the centre of the room looking quite lost - it was the Prime Minister himself. I went up to him, greeted him courteously and asked if there was any way I could help. He responded equally courteously but was clearly looking to catch the eye of someone he recognised instead of this gangling youth before him. As it happened, someone did come to his rescue and that was the end of my brief relationship with the Prime Minister of the UK, both then and at any other time. Towards the end of the evening, however, when I and my wife, Pauline, were thinking of going home, one of the more senior members of the Labour group came over to me and asked if I should like to have a drink with non-other than Barbara Castle. I was amazed but readily agreed. I don't know why we had been chosen; perhaps because we were a young handsome couple or, more likely, because there was no one else available. Both my political mentors were present, Henry and Roy, who were recognised as significant and senior members of the Labour Group. I think it was they who were responsible for the invitation. We were then led down a corridor to a smaller room where the leader of the group was with Barbara and Ted Castle. They were all consuming whiskey but I had sensibly retained hold of my beer. They were very friendly and the awesome red Queen even deigned to engage me in conversation over a recent article on economics in the Guardian which I must've mentioned, trying to impress her. She had read the article of course and asked me for my opinion, which put me directly on the spot and I attempted to answer in some halfway intelligible manner but it was probably nothing more than uninformed gibberish. Thankfully, I think she sensed my predicament and proceeded to summarise the article in ways I could understand after which we made small talk. Despite being a member of the Cabinet/shadow cabinet, Barbara Castle was a dedicated constituency MP and worked tirelessly to redress individual grievances and abuses. It was a great pity that she didn't become the first female Prime Minister. She was as gutsy and steel hard as Margaret Thatcher and I think probably more intelligent. She certainly knew more about economics. But after her White Paper *In Place of Strife*, when the Government attempted to curtail the irresponsible and often selfish power of the trade unions, she would never be supported by them to achieve the highest office.

The 70s were a dark decade in more ways than one. A split between the socialist left and the social democratic right within the Labour Party was brewing and eventually it would lead to its demise for 13 solid years of Tory rule and a period which would change the future course of this country forever. In some small way, my own political experiences reflected this turmoil. The Tory Housing Rent Act and the loss of power consequent on Blackburn becoming a district council rather than a county borough, made me more disillusioned with mainstream politics. By this time, I had become a student again obtaining a place on the B.Sc Sociology degree course at Preston Polytechnic. My shift to the left continued and, more out of curiosity than design, I found myself attending some meetings of the Socialist Workers Party, then referred to as the International Socialist Party. It was a dangerous and stupid position to be in as the Labour Party specifically prohibits being the member of another political party at the same time. As a Labour councillor, I was in an even more vulnerable and precarious position. If the press had got hold of it, I would have been mincemeat. I was seduced by activist politics, which confused demonstrations and strikes with effective democratic politics. It was only later that I came to realise that one of the core concepts of the SWP, democratic centralism, was nothing more than hypocrisy and a form of antidemocratic totalitarianism. Like a mediaeval religious organisation, this party expected its members to raise money by selling its newspaper, Socialist Worker, and contributing as much as one tenth from members' incomes. Trotsky, who had set up the party, was a former Bolshevik communist and his imprint was still powerfully exercised and evident. It took me some time to realise that not only was this form of political activity futile and fruitless but if it were to become more powerful it would be undemocratic, anti-parliamentary and dangerous.

By the time I had completed my degree course and embarked on a Post Graduate Certificate in Education, with a view to becoming a lecturer in further education, I had ceased being a Labour councillor, and a member of any party. It would be a few years yet before I returned to the Labour Party during which I was taking stock of the damage that Tony Benn had wrought within it causing the breakaway Social Democrats to emerge paving the way, for what were, from my point of view, the disastrous Thatcher years. The optimism of the Labour Movement of the 60s had been replaced by a directionless and fractured party, which contributed powerfully to the demise of the Welfare State that had nurtured me and many others of my generation since we were born. It seemed to take its toll psychologically too as I felt increasingly alienated and confused about what my values were and in which direction to go.

There are two images from that time which I retain and which effectively capture the dilemma I was in. The first was when I was still working in the insurance industry but had already applied to university and been accepted. As a member of the Council, and representing a ward with large numbers of Muslims, I was invited to a function at one of the hotels in the centre of town for which I was able to take time off work. It was to receive a well-known dignitary from Pakistan, though I have no idea who he was now. There was only one other non-Muslim present who happened to be one of the grandees of the local Labour Party. We stood milling around with the crowd nibbling at the delicious foods that had been made available. Then my rebel tendencies were expressed by wearing a suit of corduroy. I was anxious to distance myself from what I was increasingly calling a bourgeois job. I must have looked particularly out of place anywhere! When the dignitary finally arrived, the organisers set about arranging everyone around the room with what I guessed was an order of importance and seniority. My colleague in the Labour Party was almost at the very start whereas it was clear they had no idea where to place me. In the end, with some embarrassment on their part, I was placed at the very end. I was well aware of what had happened but my strong sense of egalitarianism would not allow me to become insulted by the treatment. After all I was their guest, although, on the other hand, I was a political representative and sympathetic local councillor. I suppose I could have made some trouble about this later but I didn't. I was quite naïve really and was not privy to the power brokering that went on between the local Labour Party leaders and Blackburn's Muslim community.

A completely contrasting image to this is when I was in my first year at university still living in Blackburn and on the local council. I was selling the Socialist Worker newspaper in Blackburn market. It was the week of Bloody Sunday 1972 when a peaceful demonstration by Roman Catholics in Derry, Northern Ireland, marching to demand equal social rights, were fired upon by British soldiers killing 14 people including children. The headline on the front of the paper was '**British Soldiers: Murderers**! 'Incongruously, I was dressed in an RAF greatcoat which I had taken to wearing for the past six months as it was different and a cheap purchase from the

174

town's Army and Navy Store. But I was also sporting a small lapel badge from the Chinese Embassy with a profile of Chairman Mao, (I was not a maoist but had sent for and received a copy of Mao's Little Red Book from the Chinese Embassy in London which included a photograph of him and the badge. It was one of those absurd symbolic gestures attractive to youth.) and wearing calf length suede boots. It was amazing I wasn't lynched but quite a number of people did engage me in conversation, equal numbers being supportive to those who were critical, but they were not violent or aggressive. I think that might be different today. This was the same period when I was experiencing the turmoil in my personal and family life to which I have already referred.

The Battle of Blackburn

For me, the chaotic Zeitgeist of the decade is symbolised by what has been called rather exaggeratedly, the Battle of Blackburn. I think this must have been in 1974 when I was midway through my degree course at Preston though living in Blackburn. I was a member of two political parties and I was well aware of plans to counteract a planned march in the town by a combined group of National Front and the British National Party. They had applied for permission to hold a rally in one of the town's public halls and a marching route had been agreed with the local police. As a member of the Town Council and of the Recreation Committee, which was responsible for the letting of the halls, I was opposed to allowing them that use. However, the view prevailed that whilst we might not agree with their views we could not deny them the opportunity for free speech. I think the mindset and logic would have been different today. But from within the ranks of the revolutionary socialists and student body there was a much less tolerant view which argued that they should be opposed at all costs. Before the arrival of the neo-fascists, there was a rally outside the railway station in the middle of the adjacent bus station close to Blackburn Cathedral. Thousands of students, Labour activists and members from the hard left groups, as well as a number of church groups with their families, were in attendance. I was pleasantly surprised to see one of my lecturers from the Polytechnic present and even more pleased when she took the microphone and addressed the crowd. I knew her to be a member of one of the hard left groups, probably the Workers' Revolutionary Party whose members consisted largely of academics. She gave a diatribe against allowing the racist neo-fascists to take the streets. It was almost as if she was trying to relive the person of Rosa Luxembourg in the short lived socialist German Republic of Weimar just after the First World War. She was in no mood to compromise and argued it was them or us. It was as if we held the future in our hands and the moment was ours to take or lose. She was very good at whipping up the emotions of the crowd and at the end of this peroration the neo-fascist groups emerged from the railway station. She immediately screamed urging the crowd on to refuse them the freedom of the town. There were about 20 or so police officers present and a few more tucked away in Black Marias in side streets, but these were the days before they were equipped with anti-riot gear and they seemed quite vulnerable and outnumbered in face of the anti-racists. They tried to keep the two factions apart but they were too thin a blue line and the crowd was pushed from behind through the police cordon. I was pushed along with others, some of whom were demoniacally trying to sweep the police aside to launch themselves on the racist marchers. I don't think anyone really knew what they were trying to do but the small group of skin-headed, beer-bellied demonstrators followed the directions of the police. This was away from the yelling mob, that had been waiting for them, taking a circuitous route that eventually would bring them out at their destination in another part of the town centre. There was no way they could line-up and breakthrough the people against them as they only comprised about two or three hundred. Counter demonstrators who broke through the police lines, before they were reinforced and strengthened, was about the same size as the group they were chasing and I was amongst them. There was still about 200 yards between us and they were moving fast. I looked around and recognised quite a few faces, surprised to see otherwise docile female members of the Labour Party having gone berserk, yelling and screaming, desperate to throw themselves in a violent attack on these unwelcome interlopers. After about a mile, the two groups, one pursuing and one pursued, came into contact with each other. Bricks were unleashed from each side, hurling dangerously through the air. Frantic people on both sides grabbed sticks and stones to throw and beat others with. For me it was a Damascene moment. I was completely calm but not stunned into immobility. I couldn't believe what was happening around me and all I saw were people desperately trying to assault each other. I tried to speak to some people I knew but they were in the throes of uncontrollable hysterical emotion with eyes bulging and they didn't seem to hear me. I realised then that political change could not be obtained this way. I extracted myself from the melee and walked up to where I knew there to be another counter demonstration outside the public halls, awaiting the arrival of the unwelcome guests. Here I found my senior friends in the Labour Party, who were being manhandled and told to move on by the police. Insanity seemed to rule, as this was absurd. My friend Roy, however, chairman of the Recreation Committee, and an experienced CND campaigner, was arguing the legal rights with a police inspector who then told his men to restrain themselves and not interfere with the demonstrators. I had experienced at first hand two different kinds of political action. It forced me to focus sharply, after which I parted company with the revolutionists and rejoined the parliamentarians.

A New Career

I had no idea what I should do after university but towards the end of the second year there I entered into conversation with an even more mature student than myself, who was in his late 30s. We got talking about futures and he said he was going to apply for a job in further education. I had no idea what that was as I had gone through the traditional school system and sixth form. I didn't know the difference between a college of further education, a technical college or sixth form. A number of my friends from school were attending Colleges of Education in order to become teachers but I knew I didn't want to enter primary or secondary education. This seemed a good alternative because it was dealing with older people at 16+ years and even possibly adults. I decided to explore it further and eventually decided it was a good possible future career move. During the final year, I applied for a number of posts at various types of further education colleges. Some were quite small operating out of little more than a few temporary teaching huts. I remember attending one interview which had only four demountable classrooms yet the interview panel consisted of 10 people! Fortunately I wasn't offered the job. I received three job interviews in one week after my final exams in June. One was in one of the larger Nottingham colleges, one in Wigan and one in Telford New Town. The first interview was at Telford and I was offered the job, which I accepted. I was supposed to teach General Studies and a little Sociology to GCE O and A-levels. I had never been to Telford before but it seemed remarkably congenial with its small market town in Wellington, where the college was located and in the summer of 1976 it looked especially rural, a far cry from the industrial heartlands that I had known from the age of eight years. A further attraction of the job was the offer of a newly built rented house in a nearby community called Dawley. It looked like I had arrived, but it wasn't to be quite so easy as that.

The relationship between Pauline and I was floundering. We had met when we were just 17 and 18 years of age but now we were 25 and 26 years. We had both changed but I probably more than she because of the privileged experiences I had received. She was literally left holding the baby whilst I worked full-time, plunged myself into political life and returned to university to complete my higher education. She had supported me throughout this time, even continuing to work until she gave birth and then only taking a short maternity leave of six months before we placed Ashley in a day nursery. We were able to live reasonably well on her wage as a clerk in a solicitor's office and the, by what was by today's standards, a very generous student grant. I wanted more than what I thought the relationship could offer, though I didn't know what the implications of this would be nor where it would lead. In the 70s, there was still a whiff of the 60s hippie libertarianism around and that, combined with reading sociology - which encouraged a critical appraisal of everything around in society including the family and its relationships - it was hardly surprising that I was still searching for something new. Pauline's brother, Stephen, was working as a mental health nurse in North Birmingham and he was sharing a house with a number of other colleagues. Both Pauline and I agreed that if we sold the little Victorian terraced house in Blackburn there would be a little more money for her to go and join her brother with Ashley, where there was a room available, and I would take up residence in the new house in Telford. It seemed like a good idea at the time but it wasn't very long before I was terribly miserable and missing them both.

Work was novel, interesting but very demanding. I found that the Walker Technical College's General Studies section at the time was not very well organised. There were no prepared schemes of work for new lecturers to follow and little assistance from existing staff. I had to write my own, which fortunately I was able to do from the excellent training I had received at Keele University. It was very time consuming however, and I often stayed up until midnight working from 6 to 12 a.m. planning lessons. I was just about able to keep up with the rigours of a 22 hour weekly teaching timetable, which, apart from one 2 hour evening class, consisted of unrelated separate sessions. They ranged very widely from 16 year old hairdressers to 19-year-old engineering students and one class of adult returners on a care course. I was granted no favours by the Head of Department and was expected to plunge full-time into a teaching programme that was left entirely up to me to devise. I'm happy to say that 25 years later such poor practice would not be found. It was, therefore, very stressful, which, added to the stress in my personal life, brought me to some sort of crisis. This came to a climax when I went down with food poisoning from a local Chinese takeaway and culminated in me taking two weeks off work. My mother and father came down to Telford for a few days and helped me to get back on my feet. I don't think the College expected to see me again and no one tried to find out how I was getting on. It was literally a case of sink or swim, but I swam and returned to College refreshed, determined to carry on with my new career as a lecturer, the status of which I felt proud. At the same time, I had made a decision to encourage Pauline with Ashley to come and live with me in Telford. However, this would not take place until the following summer for various reasons. I had come to reject the hippie concepts of free love and anti-family sentiments learning through experience that these were empty, dead ends. I was delighted when they finally came to join me and for a couple of years we lived a relatively happy life, moving into our own house in a semi-rural location in a little place called Doseley.

In those days, I was content to prepare my lessons well and get a buzz from having given an effective lecture or teaching session. I was still in my 20s with plenty of energy. Work was now not so draining as it had been at the beginning, I had made some very good friends amongst colleagues and we lived in what we thought at the time was a lovely house in a beautiful area. Holidays were generous and, as both Pauline and I were working, we were financially comfortable. I had vague thoughts of pursuing a masters Degree at Birmingham University but did not follow them through, probably because I had very limited ambitions at the time. It was only when I noticed another young lecturer, in hairdressing as it turned out, obtain a promotion by designing, marketing and launching a new course that I realised that was the way to get on. I resented the fact that he was not an academic but was now earning more than I was. I was clearly ambitious but this did not sit easily with my notions of socialist egalitarianism. It was a motivating factor but I didn't make full use of it at the time until I saw others equally promoted, but not for the same reason or for the valuable contribution made by the young hairdresser. The pull of the hedonistic lifestyle was quite considerable and there was a lot of latitude at that time in further education to give into it. It was only necessary to work on college premises for 30 hours a week and holidays were long with some extending into eight weeks. Often returning to work in September after two months holiday, one felt completely alienated and it took a while to re-engage with the workplace and the work pace. I regret not being more focused at that time both on my career and leisure activities. It was not until my 30s that I started to pursue cycling, camping, climbing, mountaineering and later skiing. In the holidays it was easy to grow indolent, overweight, to drink and smoke too much.

Chapter 12

The Long Slog

Autumn 1976 was the beginning of my teaching career. Two thirds of my teaching was General Studies to a broad range of day release apprentices. The remaining third was to teach Sociology O and A level GCE to full-time and part-time adult day and evening students. It is often said that teaching is a vocation rather than an occupation. I believe this to be true and I think this has sustained me throughout the past 38 years. It has been an amazingly varied career with different types of students on all kinds of courses. Whilst I may have remained at the same College throughout that time, it has never been boring, and, although it has been extremely challenging sometimes, it has been thoroughly rewarding.

Hairdressers, Engineers and Miners

In the 1970s and 80s colleges of further education were for a relatively privileged few. During the day they accommodated young people in their late teens and early 20s who had secured places on good quality apprenticeship schemes. The practice of attending one day a week or in the evening was a tradition that began in the 19th century with the various Miners and Engineering Institutes set up by of philanthropic trade unions and employers. I was employed primarily as a General Studies lecturer at the beginning, but with a Degree in Sociology I was able to teach on other courses as well. General Studies has now disappeared from the curriculum except in the form of an A level GCE subject. Defining what General Studies was and what its aims were was not at all easy to do either at the time or now. For most of the day, the students would be working on vocationally related subjects both theoretical and practical. Sometimes they would be in a classroom and at other times in a mockup of work such as a hairdressing salon or in an engineering workshop. It wasn't particularly clear why these students had to take General Studies. It seemed to be a combination of an attempt to improve their communication skills, oral and written, with a desire to broaden their general knowledge as a sort of cultural deficit model of education. The latter was clearly paternalistic originating in the well-meaning Workers' Institutes of the 19th century, which were one of the few ways by which working-class people could become better educated. The former was more functional but the nature and form of the skills involved were never very clearly spelled-out as they are now in the form of Functional Skills, attempting to compensate for the lack of having developed those skills in primary and secondary education. It is largely a forlorn task. Expecting to compensate for 10 years of statutory education, in the space of two or three years for one or two hours a week, is pushing the limits of optimism too far.

I was free to devise my own curriculum and pursue my own aims, which were implicitly, if not explicitly, political. I wanted to encourage young people to think for themselves and to be able to analyse the society in which they lived more effectively than at the level of a tabloid newspaper. But even that was idealistic and I found it particularly difficult trying to get on the same wavelength as the predominantly female hairdressing students. In the end, I settled for using astrology as a means to engage their attention and to practise some communication and numerical skills. One consolation of teaching the hairdressers was that class sizes were generally smaller than the others at around 18 to 20, whereas the engineering groups could be up to 30.

The students were generally well behaved and not too difficult to manage. I think that was because they were more able than many college students today and much more motivated to obtain City and Guilds qualifications and complete their apprenticeships. For the most part, they accepted what I and the other General Studies lecturers wanted them to do. They had to or they wouldn't pass their vocational programme.

One group of students who were notorious for their pranks amongst the staff, were the mining students. Walker Technical College had been sponsored by Walker Steel providing apprenticeship training for the area's engineering companies and the local collieries. It continued to do this until the

185

economic decline in manufacturing industries and the closure of the last remaining coal mine, Granville Colliery in the mid-1980s. After the declaration of war by Margaret Thatcher on the mining industry, the industrial landscape of the area changed dramatically. The area of Telford New Town is rich in industrial archaeology with signs of many other smaller pits at Madeley and Dawley whose legacy can still be seen in some of the older buildings like the Engineering and Mining Institutes as well as the local pubs. A number of the staff also had mining backgrounds and, whilst they taught and supported their day release students well, they were not particularly well disposed to General Studies teachers. I had the unenviable task of teaching second-year mining apprentices on the last hour of Friday i.e. from 4 to 5 PM. As the timetabling was the prerogative of the course team leader, an ex-miner himself, I was not surprised by this arrangement. Straight out of college, wide-eyed and bushy tailed, in my first session with a group of second-year mining students I wanted to teach poetry. Where was I coming from? What was I thinking? I knew better than this from my teaching practice but I thought a good dose of anarchism from Percy Bysshe Shelley himself would be good for them. They were straight talking lads who were not malicious, working class and only a few years younger than I was. I liked them and listened to their tales of the dangers of working underground and found, to my delight, they wanted to talk about politics and current affairs. They couldn't have come to a better person; both subjects were grist to my mill. After that we got on like a house on fire and I enjoyed their company and their good-natured tricks which was a reflection of their underground camaraderie that was powerfully evident in the group. They told me they chewed tobacco because underground it was forbidden to take matches or cigarettes, a grave fire risk, and being curious I asked them to show me some. Over that weekend I tried it and those of you who have experience of this archaic habit will know that you shouldn't swallow and digest it. They neglected to tell me this and consequently I spent the following day running to the loo. When I saw them again and regaled them with this, there were hoots of laughter and the bond between us was well sealed. Some of these students were extremely intelligent and sensitive, quite unlike some stereotypes of these courageous, hard-working men.

I made use of my contacts with the mining section of the College to obtain permission to visit the Colliery with a group of adult female social- care students, to whom I taught sociology on a Return-to-Work programme. It would be a completely new experience for them and, as it turned out, for me too in a different way. One day, to the complete surprise and delight of the miners on that shift, a coach load of about 25 young females between the ages of 20 and 40 years turned up at the Administration Block, where they were kitted out with helmets, batteries and lanterns. We were then led to the pit head where we were ferried down to the main road underground, which was surprisingly well lit, high and broad at that point. It did, however, undulate and in places we had to crouch low to avoid hitting the roof. We walked for a couple of miles and finally reached the main ripping face, a long, narrow gallery where we had to clamber between shiny, steel hydraulic roof supports and crawl along as best we could in front of the gleaming wet coalface. On the other side of the supports, behind us, was an empty space that we were told not to enter under any circumstances. The roof there was unsupported and waiting to collapse at any moment. The ripping machines were silent for now but it was quite a daunting and frightening experience. Overawed, we moved silently through the steel forest accompanied by some encouraging words from the miners with us aware of our anxieties. We were glad to climb out the other side. Two hours later we were back at the bottom of the main shaft waiting for the lift to return us swiftly to the safety of the surface. Once there we handed in our dockets, helmets and miners' belts and all the anxiety that had thus far been pent-up broke out in one great crescendo of laughing and joking. When we returned to the Administration Block, to the screened off shower area which had been prepared for the students, I saw a number of female faces at the windows with stern, dour looks upon them. As I entered the Block, I was confronted by two or three of the female office workers who petulantly told me to keep my 'women ' under control. They appeared to be furious that my female students had been allowed underground. I could only gape and wonder about the culture which prevailed at the pit head and the offices. There was clearly a very jealously guarded dividing line between the sexes and my visit had transgressed this.

Promotion, YOP and YTS

In my third year at the College, a position was advertised offering a promotion to someone who would lead a small research project for the Further Education Unit. Essentially, it was to work with an outside training agency to provide some form of college provision for young unemployed people who were on a government programme the ill-named Youth Opportunities Programme (YOP).This was one of a number of measures which was to be introduced in response to the growing numbers of young unemployed. A seismic shift was taking place in the UK economy, which meant that once commonly available semi and unskilled manual jobs were disappearing from the marketplace. It was a potential source of social and political instability that the government wanted to avoid at all costs. The trade unions were wary of this initiative, rightly in my opinion, as they saw the 'training/employment ' was little more than cheap labour that reduced the opportunities for real employment. A Senior Lecturer appointment was also made to act as a supervisor for the whole project and to whom I was directly responsible. She turned out to be someone with a background in English and Communications ambitious to make her mark by climbing up the greasy pole, doing whatever it took and conforming to whatever government policy dictated. She revelled in the role of liaison with the civil servants funding this project, and eventually became one of them as the Czar for further education. It was only a question of time before we clashed - our values, experience and background were totally different. My focus was much more on the young people I taught personally, whilst she remained aloof communicating with civil servants. I don't think she ever spoke to any of the trainees. Initially, I was expected to draw up a curriculum of day release teaching communication and numerical skills. I knew from my experience as a General Studies lecturer that this by itself would not be enough and I knew that these young people were even lower down the educational pecking order than the apprentices I had taught before.

After a few weeks of contact with the trainees, as they were called, my initial misgivings were confirmed. A day release programme that was far more meaningful and valuable to them would have to be provided. Whilst at College, they were provided with some practical sessions in construction trades and I discussed with the part-time lecturers, who had been expressly taken on for this purpose, what could be done. One person in particular stood out from the others, Sid Stevenson, who had considerable experience of the building industry, was intelligent and extremely personable. He said the only thing that would make sense in terms of practical relevance would be to allow them to take trade relevant training and examination i.e. City and Guilds. Sid and I became firm friends with a common aim to provide a programme which would be useful and fulfilling for these young people. It was not something that was easy to implement as the Government funders and their sycophantic supporters at the College were not keen to rock the boat, which this was seen as doing. For me, it became a point of principle and at the end of that first year I said I was going to resign from the project and go back to my old post if changes were not made. This did the trick. Sid and I were given a much freer hand to operate. Happily, the year after this coincided with the replacement of the temporary six months YOP projects with the 12 months long Youth Training Scheme i.e. YTS. It was still not a proper apprenticeship but at least our students/trainees would leave with some certification that was recognised in the industry. I redesigned the timetables so that Communication Skills formed a minimal part of it with the largest time devoted to the practical/theoretical input from the trade lecturers. The trainees loved it and came to appreciate their college days in a way that they hadn't in the first year. If it had been left to

190

Oxford educated civil servants, they would have had a full day of English and maths as a form of supplementary schooling that would have done nothing but reinforce their educational feelings of failure and inferiority.

 Meanwhile, I had enrolled on a part-time Masters course at Keele University in Social Science Research using the project as my case study. Two years later I completed it and the final report for the FEU project. The latter was archived somewhere out of sight as it did not produce the glowing endorsement of interagency work that the civil servants had wanted. In fact, it was buried because what it had shown was that such schemes for the unemployed were no substitute for real training in real work. My supervisor had already set her eyes on other routes to success and was well on the way to achieving it. I believe she became one of the youngest female principals in the West Midlands and eventually something quite senior in the civil service. I hadn't made a friend there and my career, such as it was, entered a cul-de-sac phase with me spending two more years working with the YTS trainees. Having contributed something of value to the lives of a few school rejects, I wanted to return to more academic teaching.

Pre-nurses, Carers and Social Workers

I had spent four years away from mainstream college curriculum and I now wanted to get back to it. I had successfully completed a Masters Degree in Social Science Research at Keele University and the demands of this, as well as writing up the FEU report, had satisfied my academic needs for a while. There had been a few changes at the main site and a different profile of recruitment meant that there was less demand for General Studies teaching to the kind of groups I had done before, but there was an increased demand for the teaching of sociology within a growing care section. I knew one or two of the members of staff there who were amenable to me joining their team. The alternative had been to join the English team but I had no desire to teach English GCSE. This was a fortuitous decision because a few years later there was pressure on that team to deliver Functional Skills. I had deep reservations about the educational value of this new initiative and felt relieved not to be a part of it. The Social Care section offered a much more attractive group of students and curriculum. There were 16+ students, primarily female, whose aim was to enter nursing for which they required five GCSEs and Sociology was regarded as an important subject for them. It was a one-year intensive course and the students were well motivated because of their vocational direction. Another growing area was that of social care itself which had begun to expand from what was then called PCSC, Preliminary Course in Social Care, and was intended to provide a vocational preparation for young people having left school who would seek employment in social care a more demanding and ambitious programme replaced this in the BTEC Foundation and Advanced courses, the second of which was a full-time two-year programme. All these courses provided a work placement where there would be a close link up between college and employer.

After a couple of years, I became a course tutor for one of these BTEC Advanced groups and it was a delight to be able to take responsibility for a group of students over a period of two years and see them develop as they did between the ages of 16 to 18 years. The students were not supposed to be specifically academic but some of them were definitely capable of university level study and a number of them did apply and progress to undergraduate studies at universities whilst others went into intermediary management positions in social care.

It was a pleasure to teach them and to devote my time to them extracurricularly as well. I organised walks at weekends and over the next 3 to 4 years I organised an annual week away in Snowdonia as an Outward Bound course for the students. On two of these occasions, I hired accommodation which was self catering requiring students to work in a team to buy, prepare and cook meals for themselves. I had taken a summer mountaineering training course becoming confident and qualified enough to lead students on low level walks up to 1600 feet. Anything above that or activities such as canoeing and climbing were led by instructors whom I hired in. It was for them a new and challenging experience enabling them to discover something more about themselves. It was tremendously worthwhile, although sometimes I really had to press-gang some of then to participate. Frequently, on completing the course they would say how much they'd enjoyed it. The worst moment I can remember on one of these Outward Bound courses was when I had driven the College minibus with a full group of students into Llanberis. Everyone was tired after a long journey in a noisy minibus and, as we were self catering, I decided the best thing was to get fish and chips for all. The town was very busy and there was little parking space available, so I parked wherever I could and went off with my female colleague to order the food. As you can imagine, it was such a large order that it took some time to complete and just before we were ready to return to the minibus, I looked to where I had left it to see it pulling off with all the students inside. I was flabbergasted and alarmed! When I got to the van, which was now a hundred yards away, I found one of the male students had taken it upon himself to find a better parking space as one became available and to remove the obstruction which the bus was causing. He was clearly a competent driver but I had to tell him that he was not covered by insurance and he had jeopardised potentially the whole venture, especially if there had been an accident. He was duly contrite and I insisted he promise me not to attempt to do that ever again.

In addition to post 16 school leavers, in-service courses were also provided by the Social Care section as well as a Return to Learn course for adults who had been unemployed for some time. It was on one of these courses that I was required to prepare them to make a 10 minutes oral presentation. This is a nerve wracking experience for most people the first time they do it and I had to deal with a bunch of adults whose confidence was not very great to begin with. It was essential for them to complete this task in order to obtain the full certification, so it was important to overcome their nerves. But there was one particular student who was almost physically sick at the very thought of the whole task right from the beginning. I spent some considerable time with her trying to calm her down and overcome her fears. She had prepared for it so it wasn't that she was lazy. Eventually, I agreed she could present to me alone and in that way she was able to complete the task. The irony is that she obtained employment as a Probation Officer and some years later was happy to return to College and talk to my adult students about the job she did and how she had overcome the challenges of returning to education in order to obtain a successful professional career. She had no difficulties at all giving presentations then and in fact was very good at it. She never forgot the pains I took with her and that's why she was prepared to return at my request to address students. She said that without the support I had given her she would not have been able to do what she was doing then.

Promotion and Disappointment

In 1994 a post was advertised as Senior Lecturer for GCSE, GCE and Adult Education. It required coordinating all the part-time GCSE and GCE Advanced level work in the College as well as, and this turned out to be the sting in the tail, all the non-vocational Adult Education that was provided. I already had plenty of experience with the vocational and academic work but very little with the non-vocational side i.e. flower arranging classes or foreign languages for holiday purposes. There was no longer any full-time GCSE and GCE Advanced level work remaining in the College, other than the GCSEs in English and maths which many 16 to 19 year old full-time students pursued because they had not achieved passes in these subjects whilst they were at school. At some point in the early 80s, the Shropshire Local Education Authority had decided on a policy of removing all sixth forms from the all through comprehensives and concentrating them on designated sixth form colleges. As there was already a designated sixth form College in Wellington, Telford, that was within half a mile of Walker Technical College, which later became the much larger Telford College, it was decided the former would become the academic institution and the latter the technical/vocational one. At a stroke, post 16 education in the town was segregated following traditional Tory education policy. It was a mish mash post which was effectively unviable. I was still teaching 14 hours a week and yet was expected to coordinate this unruly, conglomeration of subjects, supervising curriculum, appointing and monitoring staff, which in the case of Adult Education was wide and extensive. These classes were provided in the College itself, throughout the town and in quite a few outlying rural locations. The start of the next academic year for me was chaotic and the phone never stopped ringing as classes were found to be without a tutor, room or simply not scheduled at all with about 20 or 30 students waiting for a non-existent provision. I should have realised the idiotic situation I was in and remonstrated to senior management about the nonsensical nature of the post but I didn't and for that I must bear responsibility and it was no surprise that within six months they had decided how unworkable it was and created another Senior Lecturer post purely for Adult Education, leaving me with the GCSE and GCE. However, my potential rising star had crashed and burned almost before it got off the ground. As I swiftly learned, no one in the College at that time would support you by guiding and mentoring. You were expected to know it or make it up and implement it yourself. I wouldn't make that mistake again but it would take me some years to recover.

Nevertheless, I still had ideas and one of them, which was to bear tremendous fruit in later years, although not immediately, was to make provision for adult learners who had missed the academic boat whilst at school. I put forward to my Head of Department a plan for a part-time GCE Advanced level programme in which students could take two A-levels over a year as well as picking up some GCSEs in English and maths as necessary. It only extended to six subjects but it would be enough to be able to get someone into university as an adult returner. It ran for two full years and had a modicum of success in getting a handful of students into higher education. However, the dropout rate was quite high and not sustainable from the management's point of view so the third year there was no offer and I sat fuming outside the Principal's office demanding to know why. He refused to see me. With hindsight it is not surprising, as we were just about to enter a phase of strict number crunching and a new SS style inspection regime. Colleges of Further Education were required to produce a great deal of data and every year to carry out a SAR or Self Assessment Report. A new grading system to assess the quality of college provision was introduced and every four years a full-scale inspection would be carried out. Colleges graded as 'Needing to improve' were monitored minutely for the next two years until they began to improve. Close attention was paid to success rates i.e. examination passes and so any areas where this was weak were clearly under threat by management to be withdrawn to avoid a poor overall college grade. As most of the students on my A-level programme were adult returners and trying to take and pass two subjects in one year the results could not stand up against national averages set by sixth form colleges and schools. However, what I hadn't realised was that the Head of Department and Principal had recognised what I had set up and what successes there had been even though they could not compete nationally. There was also in another part of the college the germ of a course which was to do exactly the same but in a much more successful and efficient way. The General Studies department had launched an Access to Higher Education programme for about 25 students in collaboration with Stafford University. It offered an interesting range of subjects which included History, Economics, and English. Successful participants were guaranteed a place in a suitable undergraduate course at the University. I was not concerned with that initially but my organisational and recruitment skills had become recognised and it wouldn't be long before I was asked to contribute to this programme. It was to transform my working life.

Access to Higher Education

The following year I was asked to teach Sociology on this new adult returners programme. The year after it was added to by providing a route into nurse training requiring students to study subjects like Health Studies, Human Biology, Sociology or Psychology, English and Maths. A new university partnership was established with Wolverhampton University and specifically through the Black Country Access Federation which was centred on Wolverhampton, and surrounding towns such as Walsall and Dudley, and Birmingham. I began to become acquainted with this new network which required tutors to write their own programmes, which I was more than happy to do for Sociology. The monitoring procedures were much more rigorous than the earlier Access courses, and because of this the weaknesses in the way it was being managed at the College were exposed. The Black Country Access Federation threatened the College with withdrawing their certification unless matters were rectified immediately. Happily, I was called upon to do this and I did it so successfully that I was nominated as the programme Coordinator. I was also keen to extend the curriculum offer and increase the number of students recruited. At that time, all students had to be 21 years and over and the programme was about 50 in number. Within 2 to 3 years I had increased that to nearly 300 students with a clear vocational identity to various groups of subjects, which I think was responsible for the improved recruitment numbers. In addition to a Health Access course leading to nursing and other health-related professions such as occupational/speech therapy, radiography and midwifery, there was a general academic route for people wishing to study a range of Humanities subjects and Social Sciences at University, a Science route, a Teacher Training route and even an Art course. Recruitment was extremely successful although retention and therefore success rates were not quite so good. To some extent, this is the nature of the beast because it is a considerable challenge for a returning adult to take four or five subjects in one year full-time or over two years part-time. In addition to subjects mentioned, every student had to take English and maths which were GCSE O-level equivalents. In the end, I had to slim down the curriculum to reduce the stresses and challenge on adult learners resulting in improved retention. Overall, however, it proved to be a highly successful second chance opportunity for able and dedicated adult students over the age of 19 years and I once calculated that in a period of 20 years or so over a thousand students had successfully obtained a place at university.

The teaching team were extremely committed and there was a tremendous camaraderie for many years within the programme, especially when it became recognised as part of the mainstream vocational offering of the college. When there was a substantial restructure by the Principal, he recognised and rewarded the work that had been done and created a School or Department called MASH, an acronym for Maths, Access, Science, Humanities. I found I had been made the Head of School for all GCSE, A-level, and Access provision. I was delighted and I was also responsible for 12 other members of staff, full and part-time. We accepted the acronym of MASH joyfully and set about designating who was Hawkeye, Soft Lips, Radar and other notable worthies from the American TV series based on a field medical army unit in the Korean War. We were mostly of that generation that remembered it well. All members of staff without exception were committed to the open access/returner/2nd chance philosophy and gave 150% to the students.

You would think that teaching adults was easier than teaching post 16 students, many of whom by the late 90s were required to attend college rather than doing so on a part-time day release basis as part of a three-year apprenticeship programme. But the restructuring of the British economy had created a vast reservoir of unemployed young people who, had it not been for the response of colleges of further education, would have been aimlessly wandering the streets and posing a threat to the social order. Nonetheless, they were still biding their time until they reached the ages of 18 or 19 years when they had to take their luck in an ever diminishing and hostile labour market. Some of them were recruited to the Access programme but these were the lucky ones. Some of the vocational courses were extremely good, able to enthuse young people with confidence in themselves and hope for the future. But not all could achieve this high standard and those, especially the less academic or vocationally undemanding, were regarded very much as the earlier youth training schemes had been i.e. worthless.

However, teaching adults created its own challenges. The students were of all ages from their early 20s to the mid-to-late 40s and sometimes even older. They came with a range of life experiences, social class and ethnicity. They included single mothers on the outlying estates of Telford in some of the most deprived areas who were striving to improve their life chances and those of their children. Staff couldn't help but admire the determination to overcome the obstacles life had put in their way from birth. I can remember a number of young mums, often vilified in the Tory press as benefit scroungers, who went on not only to pass the course but even to excel obtaining excellent degrees at University. Some even made it despite being pregnant with their second or third child. Others were young men in their early 30s who had become unemployed in a declining engineering industry who were seeking to change their careers by going into nursing or social work. Some were middle-class whose confidence and self-image had been undermined by lives dedicated to rearing children - lives stunted by the stigma of motherhood. There were also those from backgrounds which were a little more unusual or unconventional such as the drug addicts, prostitutes, petty criminals and mentally ill. A few such students could create tremendous difficulties because of the needs they had but course tutors threw themselves into supporting them as strongly as they could.

There were successes and failures. I remember one of each. I continued to teach Sociology even whilst managing the programme and I recall one young, female Asian student in her mid-20s who wore a head covering but whose views were stridently feminist and Marxist. She was highly intelligent, articulate and well read. She was attractive with a forceful character but sensible and sensitive of others around her. After three months she simply stopped coming and though I made enquiries after her, I never saw her again. It was as if she had disappeared from the face of the earth. Now with hindsight, I fear the worst might have happened to her, but in those early days before Safeguarding Panels and the revelation of female abuse within some Muslim communities, we had no structures by which I could take it further. Much more recently, there was the incident when I was keeping an eye on a class in an IT room when the tutor was absent due to illness. It was adjacent to my office and I could pop in and out as required. The class was a Pre-Access course which was intended to provide a foundation to allow weaker students to progress to the full Access programme. As I went round the room, I noticed one young man in his mid-30s staring curiously at a blank piece of paper so I sat down to see if I could assist. I believe their task was to research a topic and write an essay on it. When I asked him how he was going on, he shoved the blank piece of paper towards me and said it was all there. I didn't quite know how to take this. I didn't know whether he was having fun with me or whether he was being serious. He certainly looked deadly earnest. When I quietly told him that I couldn't see anything, he told me it was written in Dragon's blood. I was stunned and realised there was something going on here more than a joke. I asked him to come into my office so we could discuss it and I spent an hour with him listening to what he had supposedly written. He was extremely well read in philosophy quoting Schopenhauer, Karl Marx, Freud, Nietsche and so forth. I didn't press the matter further then but when his tutor returned, she confirmed that he was somewhat odd although by no means any trouble in class. A little later she told me he had stopped attending. A whole year later, however, I met him again at a recruitment session for the Access programme. This time he had his wife with him who was also applying to the same course, the one I tutored called Access to Welfare for people intending to pursue a career in social work or social care. He was very contrite about the incident of the previous year. His wife explained that he was in fact schizophrenic and at that time had not been taking his medication. When they saw me, it was evident they thought their chances of getting onto the course were absolute zero. But I told them they, or rather he specifically, would be treated like every other application and he was. It was a perfectly good one and I saw no reason for refusing him admission. When I saw them at the first class, they both expressed their profound gratitude. They worked very hard, hardly missing a lesson, and at the end of the Access course progressed to the Foundation Degree programme, also available at the College. I had the supreme satisfaction two years later of seeing them graduate successfully. With his wife's support, and despite having two young children, they had both passed two very challenging courses. What a success!

Chapter 13

Trade Unionism

'**M**r Conway, I'm told that you are often late for your classes.'
This was to be my initiation by management into my role as a trade union branch officer. When I arrived at the College in 1976, I found it had an active trade union branch. As I was often outspoken at branch meetings, before very long I was elected to the branch committee and a year or so later was elected to be Branch Secretary. It was shortly after this that I was summoned to the Principal's office where an attempt was made to intimidate me and put me firmly in my place. However, my character does not react well to such strong arm tactics and I usually end up seeing red and come out fighting, which is what I did on this occasion. I challenged the Principal to say who had made this accusation, which he ignored, so I followed it up with a strong statement to the effect that I took my duties seriously and was never late for class or my students, which was true. He had the Vice-Principal with him at this time, presumably for some kind of moral support. The fact that

I was in my mid twenties, a new member of staff and a primary grade lecturer, was evidently not sufficient to give them all the confidence that resided in their offices. Furthermore, this particular person was a good 6 inches taller than I was. I knew what they were up to and I told them so in no uncertain terms with my eyes blazing. Jumping up from my seat, I adopted a confrontational pose and waited for them to respond. They both visibly shrank before my eyes. Having said my piece, I left the office and slammed the door. That would be my attitude towards senior management for the next 20 years in my role first as Branch Secretary and then as Chairman. I had brought with me from my experience in a northern industrial town my class-based and conflict ridden politics as well as my Marxist/socialist views. I was not going to be a pushover especially when I perceived injustice wherever it might appear. I was never well predisposed to the management caste because I believed many of them to be incompetent and not worth the extra money they were paid. The reason many of them were in that position was because of sheer good luck, being in the right place at the right time, or because they had such a useful servile attitude to their seniors that they were slotted into better paid senior positions whenever they became available. I have always held the opinion that the main business of an educational institution is to teach and those who don't are hardly in a fit position to lead those who do. I was incensed generally by these lazy individuals who arrived at the office about 8:30 AM and left sharply at 5 PM without taking any work home with them, such as marking and preparation. I believe the best institutions are those where the senior management continue to do some teaching themselves.

When I began my career in Further Education, the main trade union for lecturers was the National Association of Teachers in Further and Higher Education (NATFHE). In the early years of the 70s it had capitalised, like many trade unions, on the economic and social unrest of the period to win for itself and its members considerable improvements not only in pay but also in conditions of employment. When I began my trade union career, the main aim was to ensure that these freshly won gains were recognised and implemented fully. Our Bible was The Silver Book, which contained all these nationally agreed rights but which were far from being recognised in many colleges, so it was for each branch to take action to ensure they were. When the Silver Book conditions were fully recognised, the lecturer's job was much easier and more fulfilling as one could devote one's energies totally to the business of education i.e. of developing young, and not so young, minds. In all the years I have spent in Further Education, my experience has been that this was a very lowly placed aim surpassed by a bureaucratic and servile commitment to the latest government folly. When I first started teaching, lecturers had to teach 22 hours a week and be present on college premises for at least 30 hours. This may not seem very much to the outsider but when you consider that one hour of teaching may involve one hour of preparation and one hour of marking, and sometimes much more, one may come to accept that 22 hours could easily exceed 60 hours a week. It was common for managers to try to pressure lecturers to teach more hours, which was extremely stressful for the individual and ultimately detrimental to the quality of the teaching and learning experience. It was not only important to monitor the number of hours being taught in a week or over a year, but also to watch out for other types of bad practice, which were a result of poor management that also created more stress for the individual lecturer. These were abuses like back-to-back classes so that there was not even a break for a drink or toilet visit over four or five hours. Another pressure was to timetable lecturers for more than two evenings a week. Many of these practices have re-emerged unfortunately among some occupations where zero hour contracts are to be found e.g. caring. The trade unionist cannot rest on his or her laurels but must be forever vigilant. It is a continual struggle between labour and capital for power and control, which ebbs and flows over the decades. Individuals were on occasion bullied by managers and this is where I as Branch Secretary would intervene to protect them negotiating directly on their behalf. Sometimes it was necessary to bring in a full-time union officer and even to take legal action. It is amazing how hierarchies can breed bullies and and submit the strongest individual to intolerable stresses and strains which can contribute to mental ill-health. I have seen too many examples of this. To stand up against the institutional power of managerial hierarchies and all that they can threaten, requires strength and a certain attitude of mind which a collective like a trade union can provide.

One of the first battles I can remember having was over the issue of part-time lecturers. It was union policy that when someone was employed on a part-time contract, and it was renewed after 12 months on the same basis, it should become a full-time post deserving a full pension, sick pay and holiday rights. But this did not always happen. In such instances, the case had been established that there was a longer term need and people should be provided with the security of full-time contracts to enable them to get on with their lives, not wondering if from year to year they would be re-employed.

Again, in today's zero hour contract environment, there seems to be wide acceptance of this practice. There were half a dozen lecturers in this position working on government schemes in YTS and I had worked alongside them at the beginning so I was keen to do something to redress this abuse. I had a long correspondence with senior management but could get no joy out of them. They would just not commit to taking them on again the following year until right at the last moment, still on part-time contracts. In the end, I decided the only thing to do was to take the management to an Employment Tribunal. I and a colleague, who taught trade union studies, made the application, collected the evidence and presented it to the tribunal. The Principal was furious at this action but was even more furious when he and the College lost the case incurring a considerable fine to be paid as well as compensation and re-employment of the lecturers concerned. It was a great victory for the branch and it strengthened the union considerably at the time enlarging the membership so that it accounted for at least 90% of the teaching staff. The Tribunal was conducted like a court case and I was interrogated and cross examined by lawyers for the College management. It was difficult to say at the time what the outcome would be and we had to wait a few months for the judgement. Apparently, however, it came down to good record keeping and correspondence which had been submitted to the Tribunal. This documentary evidence proved to them that the union had given management every opportunity to abide by the legislation, which they had singularly failed to do. I believe my name became a byword for something unpleasant in the Principalship and it is hardly surprising therefore that my career went into the doldrums for quite a few years until a new Principal arrived who had a very different style and outlook.

At first, I thought I and the new Principal would get along fine. He was only a few years older than me and was another northerner. However, events beyond us both conspired against this. The first was his attempt to introduce a system of staff appraisal, which was being pushed by managements throughout the country at the instigation of the Inspectorate. This was resisted by the unions because it went hand in glove with attempts to introduce performance-related pay. It was an American management philosophy used as a means of employee control, especially in the private sector. However, British trade unionists saw it for what it was, a means to divide and control the workforce. It was particularly odious in the context of education where the aim is not to increase profits for shareholders or produce more widgets than the competitors, but to develop something much more complex, a fully rounded and educated individual that was a product of their whole educational experience and not a consequence of one single teacher. Furthermore, the idea of motivating teachers by monetary means to do the best for their pupils or students flies in the face of their vocational professionalism, especially when one teacher may be rewarded more than another with the same experience for doing exactly the same thing. It is a one-dimensional management tool which has a tendency to be abused by managers, pitting workers against each other.

I led the counter-attack from the union side and the Principal's softly-softly approach ended in failure. All of this, however, was overtaken by a much more serious challenge that emanated from Government. This was the Tory policy of privatising the public sector and running it along ideological market lines. Further education colleges were to be made independent of LEAs and given a budget to run themselves, for which they would tout annually direct to the Department for Education. Colleges were expected to make savings by introducing a whole range of new employment conditions for staff. Each was charged with trying to implement, with or without trade union involvement, new contracts which were a complete denial of the Silver Book and national bargaining. For years and even today, lecturing staff may be paid quite different amounts according to where they happen to work. It was expected that staff would certainly have to work longer hours, have fewer holidays and get less or no recognition for any additional duties they might have to do. It was a wholesale war and for two years that is what it felt like. Unless we accepted the new contracts there would be no anti-inflationary wage rises. When this didn't seem to be working, certainly at Telford College, management resorted to bribery offering £1000 to anyone who would go on the new contracts. I think half a dozen did so and were treated as pariahs by the rest of the staff. From time to time, a union negotiating committee would sit down with the management and try to come up with an acceptable compromise but of course any compromise was going to be a departure from what we already had so there was little incentive other than the gradual attrition of no wage increases year on year which were beginning to seriously undermine our living standards. It placed a great burden on everyone and I know at least two lecturers who went off on extended sick leave as a result. Others left the profession, but most were not in a position to do that and eventually after three or four years there was a very slow drift to accepting the new reality. I felt quite bitter at the time that the national trade union had not taken a stronger lead and given more help to the individual branches. We felt unsupported, stranded and isolated. But we were not coalminers and we could not hold the country to economic ransom. I had taken the opportunity during this time to apply for and obtain a senior lectureship and shortly after I did, I joined a College Managers' union. I was very much of the opinion that the lecturers' union had been found wanting and had let its members down. I believe it had shown little loyalty in the end to its membership and so I saw no reason in return to show it any loyalty. I was under no illusion about the new union and refused to get involved in branch politics as I had in the previous one. I looked upon it as a means of obtaining legal aid and representation if it were needed.

A related issue to the contract one was that of some kind of staff appraisal scheme, that was inevitably introduced, becoming part of an internal quality process requiring annual teaching observations. The final step was to be the introduction of performance -related pay but that had not happened happily by the time I had left the college. There was a halfway scheme that had been introduced which invited lecturers to apply for an extra increment if they could prove they were 'good 'teachers, based on a good or excellent annual grading in the teaching observation process. I know that in many secondary schools the introduction of performance -related pay has gone much further than this but I do wonder whether it has improved the teaching and learning that takes place? Having carried out many observations myself and been observed many times as well, I am highly sceptical of the value of this unless it is done in a supportive and cooperative atmosphere. However, I fail to see how this is possible when it is linked to pay. Having gone through many inspections, especially as a manager as well as a lecturer, I am well versed in the obscurities and absurdities that from time to time have been adopted, discarded and then readopted. The last scheme which I experienced at the College, introduced to satisfy the inspectors, was a hundred-point checklist of what the observer should make a judgement on in a one-hour teaching session. I believed it to be practically impossible to do and effectively it skewed the whole focus of good teaching to what were essentially non-teaching outcomes. It is one thing to want to improve one's teaching but it is quite another to be forced to conform by jumping over a set of hurdles that corresponds to a checklist and assumes that good teaching is absolute and can only take one form. Teachers are individuals with their own personalities and styles which they use to establish a positive and workable rapport with their students. It is what I refer to as the black box. If one can measure what goes into the box and compare it with what comes out, hopefully a vast improvement, then there is no need to go tinkering around in the box itself.

Trade union activity was an important part of my life for more than 25 years. It was stressful and yet I had to do it. Had I avoided the stress would this dreadful condition i.e. MND have been any different or perhaps not even have affected me at all? Who can say? I have lived my life as I thought fit and believe that most of the things I did were positive, hopefully for me and others too.

Chapter 14

Remaining Sane

W ork is a central part of many people's lives and for fortunate people like me it can be richly rewarding. Keeping abreast of new knowledge, developing young minds and helping people to fulfil their ambitions are important benefits from teaching. It makes life worth living and one feels fulfilled. I know that is not the case for everyone and even so, work-life can be a source of great stress, or distress, and it is crucial to have some way of maintaining the balance between work and non-work. It's also very much about sharing one's life with others so that one can maintain a good socio-psychological equilibrium. I had a number of interests, hobbies and activities which allowed me to do this.

Walking, Climbing and Mountaineering

I have always been a keen walker even during my dissipated, late teenage years and early 20s, but it really wasn't until my early 30s after meeting Carol this began to increase significantly. I bought a copy of William Poucher's guide to walking in Wales and the relevant maps to go with it, giving me the confidence to strike out into the incredible beauty of the Welsh mountains. I could use a map and compass because I had learnt these skills as a Boy Scout. We spent many wonderful weekends driving into the glory of Wales to bag a mountain or two in Snowdonia, the Berwyns, the Harlech Dome or Cader Idris. With our growing skills and fitness, we also ventured into the Lake District where we spent a two-week holiday walking many of the classic routes and peaks. A little later we extended this to Scotland and in particular to the mountains around Glencoe and Fort William, It was on one of these occasions that we met a fascinating character called Patrique, who was French and working as a mental health nurse in the UK. It wasn't so usual in the 80s to come across European nationals living and working in Britain and we soon befriended him, discovering that he was in the process of taking his Scottish Winter Mountaineering certificate. He was quite keen to come along with us to practise his guidance and instructional skills.

One day, we ventured into the Lost Valley to the north of the Three Sisters in Glencoe. It was winter and the snow was thick everywhere, covering boulders and tracks with most of the streams iced over. We were well equipped with crampons I had borrowed from College and newly purchased ice axes, which we didn't yet know how to use properly. Patrique was quite keen to teach us and we spent the afternoon learning how to do ice axe breaks, throwing ourselves backwards and sideways down a steep slope. It was exhilarating. The following day Patrique offered to take us on a grade two or three snow climb, which was to be up a narrow gully on the lonely Sentinel, entrance to the Glencoe Valley, Buachaille Etive Mor. It was quite a formidable challenge given its steepness in places but we were all roped up with Patrique in the lead. Fortunately, the snow was in great condition and, even though it became steeper and steeper towards the top, our ice axes held firm and our crampons provided us with extra security. It was marvellous to complete the climb and emerge almost at the summit of the mountain. I and Carol had been hooked by the adventure and we wanted more of it. With two other friends, we would frequently leave Telford as soon as we could after 4 pm on Friday and drive all the way up to Glencoe often arriving just in time for last orders at the only pub in the area, the Claichaig, where we refreshed ourselves with a few pints and bridies, a sort of Scottish pasty. Most times we were able to obtain accommodation in the local bothy or climbing hut, but on one miserable occasion there was no room available, except for a primitive shelter at the back of the pub. This turned out to be nothing more than a chicken coop, which we could hardly stand up in, but it did keep most of the cold and bad weather from us. The following day, before we did anything else, we secured B&B accommodation as close to the walking area as we could. We weren't going to spend another night with the smell of chicken shit in our nostrils.

With our new-found confidence and a modicum of winter-mountaineering experience, we felt ready for the French Alps. We had joined the British Mountaineering Association to obtain the necessary insurance cover happily finding that membership entitled us to a discount at alpine huts and on the Chamonix bus, which travelled overnight from Victoria Bus Station in London. It was a fairly gruelling trip but we were young and fit. We had all our equipment with us such as climbing hardware as well as a tent and small stove. What more did we want? I think the answer was probably sleep and rest at altitude but we couldn't wait to get high. There was a cable car not far away from where we were camping in Argentiere and the following morning we decided to head up the mountain by taking it. It whisked us rapidly from about five thousand feet to ten and a half thousand feet. The previous afternoon we had spent equipping ourselves with the latest crampons and ice axes and other pieces of equipment such as pitons, which we were now eager to test. We had also lashed out and purchased the latest, plastic boots for mountaineering which resembled ski boots.

It was surprisingly warm at the Grand Monte Col and there were quite a few people milling around, sitting at tables and sipping beers or Coca-Cola. I couldn't wait to get my gear on and hadn't noticed the slight woozy feeling that was beginning to creep over me. Crampons in place, climbing helmet fixed, and ice axes ready I turned towards the snow slope that led up to a crevasse which was 4 feet wide at the top that would have to be crossed before the steeper snow wall could be climbed to the main ridge. I began trudging towards a point 200 yards away but after about 10 minutes came to a full stop. My head was swimming, I had a raging migraine, I was desperately thirsty and my feet, or rather legs, felt as though they had iron weights attached to them. I couldn't go on. Carol was just behind me seemingly unaffected but she came to my assistance as soon as she saw my state helping me back to one of the benches near the refreshment cabin. I realised at once I was suffering from altitude sickness and was in a fairly bad way. We had no choice but to descend and spend a day or two acclimatising before we attempted anything this high. Eventually we did acclimatise, climbing to over twelve and a half thousand feet and staying overnight in the Argentiere hut before leaving at 2 a.m. in the morning to tackle the peak. This in itself was quite an expedition and provided us with an unexpected experience. In the dark using the light of our head torches, we climbed up to the first glacier which we then had to cross to gain a higher one to make the main ridge. There were a number of other climbers in the area roped up as we were as security against one of us falling down a crevasse. However, this glacier was mainly ice with little snow covering as it was in July and we could clearly see where most of the crevasses were, but what we hadn't expected, although we were aware of such possible dangers, were the erratic rockfalls, some of which we could see as large as footballs bounding down the slope in front of us. We steeled ourselves against this to travel as quickly as we could across this exposed area. Just before we reached what we considered safety, a huge boulder appeared out of the darkness bouncing 20 feet away from us going completely over our heads. The boulder must have been at least 10 to 15 feet high. If it had hit us, I wouldn't be writing this now. It shook us severely but we carried on determined to reach our goal. We were fit and climbing strongly even over taking a number of other climbers using our ice axes and crampons like professionals on the ever increasingly steeper slope. About 200 yards from the summit, the sun came up and we could see the mountains all around in this wonderful high-level world. But we could also see something else. There was a large black bank of cloud moving swiftly in our direction from the south-east. The mountaineer's worst fear - a storm was heading directly towards us and it would be fatally negligent to carry on, so we turned around and headed down as fast as we could noticing that all the others were doing the same. We then returned to the larger, lower glacier and threaded our way between the crevasses back to the security of a mountain track where we could rest and take off our equipment and replace our heavy plastic boots with lighter footwear. We had made the right decision as for the next two days the heavens opened at that level and we sheltered as best we could in our little Vango tent. There were compensations such as spending time in the local bars or dining well in a rustic French restaurant, which was a little on the pricey side but which fortunately accepted plastic.

One of the most memorable and enjoyable treks that we made in the Alps was in Austria. This time our son, Alex, was with us and a dear Austrian friend of ours, Christina. Alex was only eight years old at the time but he was quite used to accompanying us on long walks and was incredibly strong for his age. This particular route was a circular one called the Gosau Kam and was situated at the north east end of the Dachstein plateau with its all year-round glacier, but we were not going to challenge that on this occasion. It began with a cable car ride to the major ridge where we then had a two hour walk in to an alpine hut where we had made reservations for the night. There was hardly anyone there and we had a whole dormitory to ourselves. In the morning we set off reasonably

218

early at 8 am with the intention of circling round the main crest of the ridge and eventually coming to another alpine hut that was remotely situated on this side of the massif. The day began extremely well. The weather was absolutely beautiful and we could admire the alpine meadows and flowers in the pure azure blue atmosphere of the Alps. We had about a 6 to 8 hour walk ahead of us and in parts the path was narrow and steep but it was not dangerous. There was a tiny private Alpine chalet en route which sold refreshments where we discovered the delights of a very refreshing, non-alcoholic Austrian drink called Almdudeler. We made good time and arrived at the large Alpine hut by mid- afternoon. It was busy with walkers pouring in from all directions. We ordered the hot food available and then relaxed outside on the terrace where we noticed some ominous grey clouds drifting in from the West. Checking the weather forecast we discovered that a powerful thunderstorm was going to engulf the area for the next two days. We would be stranded, we realised, for at least the next two days in this hut unless we did something fast. After some reflection, we decided we could try to complete the walk and rendezvous back at our base with Christa's partner, Heinz, who hadn't joined us because he didn't like heights. The return journey required us to climb over a high pass of over six thousand feet. I reckoned we could make it before the bad weather hit us and I was right. However, the entire journey was another eight hours walking, some of which was quite steep climbing. It was very beautiful, especially as we threaded our way through a series of limestone erratics but it was very taxing for one so young as Alex. I had to create some kind of alternative focus to the continual trudging along this path so I began to relate to him one of his favourite tales, the Lord of the Rings, which I embellished and altered over the next eight

219

hours. It did the trick and he was lost in that wonderful fantasy world of Tolkien's for the rest of the journey. Just as we reached our tents, darkness had fallen and so had the torrential rain which the storm had brought. We went to the nearest pub ordering a meal and as it arrived, Alex took two or three spoonfuls and collapsed fast asleep in his dinner. We arranged a little bed for him by the table whilst we drank and ate. It had been a remarkable feat of endurance for Alex but it hadn't done him any harm and the following morning he was fresher than any of us. The resilience of children is remarkable.

Climbing

As we completed more and more routes in the Alps, some of which required scrambling over rock, I wanted to improve my skills to do even more alpine routes. The next step really was to start rock climbing, so over the next year I began acquiring the necessary knowledge and equipment to handle ropes and climbing hardware. There was a lot that could be done within a short distance of home and I remember in particular cutting my teeth on an outcrop near Pontesbury, the Earl's Rock Reserve. As my confidence grew I began looking for people with whom to climb. Pregnancy seemed to have dulled Carol's appetite for this dangerous activity but until then she had been quite audacious. I launched out with a colleague of mine, Crispin, seeking out routes in the local quarries and even tackling the easier climbs in Snowdonia, near Lake Ogwyn. Eventually, I joined the Telford and Wrekin Mountaineering Club where I learned a lot more about rope work and climbing techniques.

I became a crag rat. I was away climbing every other weekend in summer and every season, weather permitting, saw me in Snowdonia climbing a crag or a classic mountain rock route. It could be a dangerous business but I was always very careful and enjoyed balancing the risks associated with the whole sport. I found that climbing was so singularly demanding, requiring total concentration on route finding, that it took my mind off everything else, especially the stresses which were accumulating at work. But the dangers were never far away and I was abruptly reminded of these one weekend when a small group from the Club arranged an outing in the Snowdon area. Crispin, my climbing partner at the time, and I had decided to tackle a long classic mountain route on the east face of Lliwedd. It would take us nearly 8 hours to complete and then we had to walk off which would take another hour and a half. The other group of five had decided to go scrambling, which means climbing on rock without necessarily having the protection of ropes because the terrain is not as steep or challenging. We knew the group was in the area but we had no contact with them because we were in a completely different part of the range and were not in contact by phone - the magical age of solitude that prevailed prior to mobile phones. That night after returning home, I received a call from the other group's leader's wife wondering where he might be. It transpired that there had been a tragic accident and that the leader, Emrys, had fallen to his death. He had grabbed a piece of rock which simply broke off plunging him 300 feet down a ravine. There was nothing that could be done for him. We were all absolutely stunned and mortified. The irony is that he wasn't even climbing with ropes because he shouldn't have needed to and this was nothing to do with a mistake he made but is what is termed an objective factor i.e. the fault lay in the rock, not the climber.

Danger knocked again a couple of years later when I was climbing in the Ogwyn area. Nick, a new climbing partner, and I had just completed a 300 feet classic called Hope and I began a shorter, but more difficult, extension climb known as Direct Route. I had climbed about 30 feet up placing protection in a groove. The next phase was to surmount the groove and carry on, but I found that no matter what I did, I just couldn't get up this obstacle. Eventually, I decided to take an alternative line which lay to the left and presented a steep, nearly vertical face of 30 feet. I had only one piece of protection in, which was in the impossible groove, so I decided to leave it where it was. I launched out onto the wall and found that though it was thin i.e. very little to hold onto, I could actually move up it until I reached a ledge onto which I simply needed to mantle shelf and safety. However, I was stuck! The rope wouldn't move. It was jammed because of the acute angle I had created by climbing the face. Desperately, I held on with one hand and pulled with the other, but the rope simply wouldn't BUDGE. I couldn't get the rope to shift at all. I knew it wouldn't be long before I ran out of strength so I warned my partner I was going to fall and I did. Fortunately, I fell vertically for 30 feet turning upside down in my half harness climbing belt, but the protection held fast. Not only did I avoid the ledge on which my partner stood, I also somehow didn't collide with any protruding rocks. I was extremely lucky because if the protection had failed I would have plunged a further 500 feet down the face up which we had climbed earlier. I was very shaken and there was no way that either of us were going to continue climbing up the route, so we pulled the rope through abandoning the piece of protection which had held so well, descending safely. I still continued to climb after this incident but for a while my confidence had been shaken and I was not quite so daring as I had been.

Skiing

Carol and I were late-comers to skiing because we preferred to go mountain walking even in winter and skiing was so much more expensive. I had taken a beginners' course many years ago on the dry ski slope in Telford but I hadn't progressed very far from the standard beginners' snowplough. However, friends who ran a ski business on the Italian- French border in the Haute Savoy encouraged us one year to go out and join them for a week. After that we were smitten. We always loved the high Alpine atmosphere and for five solid days there were perfect blue skies with excellent snow conditions, at least for beginners. It was ideal for developing our technique and discovering we could stay upright for more than a few minutes. By the end of the week we were able to ski down green and blue runs imbuing us with a feeling of well earned success. After that, we tried to go every year, although because my job did not allow me to take holidays whenever I liked, it was often at the end of the season i.e. late May or early April before we could go. Further education does not usually allow staff to take half term February holidays. Sometimes we were lucky and the snow was in great condition but sometimes it was sparse, icy and had to be refreshed overnight with the use of snow cannons. We became quite proficient confidently skiing all the red runs and making expeditions over the border from France into Italy to well-known Olympic runs at Sestriere. Before my last skiing holiday, I had acquired sufficient confidence to tackle the more extreme black runs although I sometimes finished up like Eddie the Eagle sprawled in the snow somewhere. These were great times and we thoroughly enjoyed immersing ourselves in the food and culture of France and Italy. The last time I went skiing, however, which was about a year and a half before I was diagnosed, I began to experience some difficulties with trying to maintain parallel skis. My left leg kept wandering out and this significantly affected my progress often causing me to take falls where the year before I had skied quite competently. With hindsight, I can now see this was a result of drop foot and a hidden early sign of MND. I did take quite a few falls that season and I sometimes wondered later whether one of these may have contributed to the onset of my condition. But it is probably unlikely as none of these led to serious injury. The following year, even before I was diagnosed, it was clear that I wouldn't be able to undertake a skiing holiday because of the difficulties I was having walking. I encouraged Carol, nonetheless, to take a holiday and she did so with our friends and Alex. It was very disappointing for me and for her too because we always enjoyed, wherever possible, doing things together.

Cycling

Another activity which we very much enjoyed was exploring the countryside by bicycle. Ever since Alex was a toddler, I had strapped him behind me on a bike and when he was a little older himself, he had his own touring bike which we had bought in Austria one year when we visited our friends, Christina and Heinz. They were also keen cyclists and on many occasions over the past 25 years we have cycled from their lovely home near the Czech border in north-west Austria down to the Danube. It is an easy cycle ride down and on reaching the river, there is a purpose-built cycle track which runs along on alternating sides of the river all the way from Bavaria to Hungary. We could pick up part of this track and cycle pleasantly along one of the most beautiful sections of this most important of rivers in Europe, where it passed through a deep winding gorge, heavily wooded on both sides. This part of it is known as die Schlange or snake as it curves in graceful bends for about 8 miles. After that we had to climb strenuously up to return to our starting point. When Alex was older and stronger we planned longer routes cycling from Passau to Linz in one day. This was great fun as it required taking a small ferry to the other side of the river, the southern bank where we would travel for miles through beautiful pines until we came to one of the many bridges over the river enabling us to crossover and carry on. One of the most delightful trips that we took along the Danube was from Linz to Vienna when we stayed at B&B accommodation en route for two nights, passing through a very beautiful vine growing area called the Wachau. This is the place that Richard the Lion Heart was incarcerated for a year before being found by his trusty servant Blondel. He had to pay a king's ransom to be released, a sum of money which almost bankrupted his kingdom. At the beginning of the journey, we weren't sure whether we would be able to continue because of the torrential rain that suddenly engulfed the area and threatened to flood the river breaching

225

its banks on either side. But after a couple of hours or so it stopped raining and we carried on. It is an extraordinary sight when you draw near to the ancient city of Vienna, in what is referred to as Lower Austria, because you have to thread your way through a delightful collection of rustic sheds and huts looking very much like an English allotment, only larger. They are in fact summer chalets where the Viennese can escape the heat of the summer and are rather like Russian dachas. As you approach the city, they appear to get larger and larger and are clearly owned by the wealthier inhabitants of the region.

Another wonderful cycling tour we made with our Austrian friends was from quite a high point in the Austrian Alps, in the Hoher Tauern range, starting at one of the longest waterfalls in the European Alps, Krimmler Wasser Falle. It took careful planning because we had to take three trains to get ourselves and our cycles to the starting point. The last part of the train journey was a rack and pinion mountain train which was quite small but powerful. The ingenious thing about this was how the cycles were stored along a rail provided with what resembled meat hooks from which they hung vertically by the front wheel. It was then secured by a belt and the whole thing was absolutely secure against the swaying of the little train.

These were the major cycling tours that we made abroad although we often took our cycles to France where there are also some excellent routes. For example, one of our favourites followed the River Loire that ran all the way to La Rochelle.

We also made many tours in the UK, one of the longest and most memorable was from Ilfracombe to Plymouth. This incredibly varied route skirts Dartmoor after winding along the

226

Tarka Trail which crosses the estuary at Barnstable and through a beautiful nature reserve. We spent three nights in B&Bs en route and it was just as well we did. There was torrential rain when we reached Tavistock from where we cycled steeply up to contour along an old railway line to a very welcome hostelry that was full of people enjoying the bank holiday weekend. We had fortunately made reservations. Thereafter, after a few ups and downs, it was all the way downhill crossing the River Plym into Plymouth. It was a coast-to-coast route that was immensely picturesque taking in two coastlines, Dartmoor and various other heights. It was all the more remarkable that we actually completed this classic trek. A week before I had stopped very suddenly on my own bike and Carol had ploughed into the back of me, falling heavily to the ground and, as it turned out, sustaining a hair-line fracture of her left wrist. She wore a brace and had a pocketful of painkillers. Nothing stops my Carol. From home we were used to cycling in many directions. For example, into Shrewsbury where we knew a safe route that took us in via the River Severn all the way into the centre of town. It took over an hour but it was well worth it. Many a time on Saturdays when the weather was looking promising, we cycled from home to Church Stretton, a distance of about 18 miles. Again, we knew how to avoid the busy roads taking small roads through the Upper Severn Valley. In Church Stretton, Carol enjoyed herself wandering around the secondhand shops whilst I went to the butchers or the off-licence. Our panniers were always full when we returned home. It was a great day out. One of the last times I remember taking that route, I recall Carol and I used to race each other up the steep road from the bridge over the River Severn to see who could arrive puffing and panting to be the first home. I don't remember which one of us won this time but when I threw myself down on the bed to rest for a while, I had the most strange sensation, which I can only explain as every muscle in my body feeling as though it was screaming. Was this another sign of things to come?

Cooking and Mushrooms

As for many people I suspect, I found preparing, cooking and eating food was a tremendous way to relax, especially on a Friday evening after a hard week's work. It was usually accompanied by a glass or two of wine at the same time and I had to be careful to pace myself so as not to drink all the wine before the meal was on the table. I had always been interested in making my own meals since my 20s but this grew considerably as I settled down and didn't feel the need to go clubbing, which I have never done, or pub crawling, which was a pastime I used to engage in when I was younger. Carol is a good cook too but she was always very willing to allow me to experiment with various recipes which I liked to do. My favourite dishes are normally taken from Italian, French or Austrian and German recipes. This goes hand-in-hand with my appreciation of mushrooms or mycology, which I have also developed over the last three decades. I go in search of the deliciously edible fungi but it's also very useful to have a knowledge of the non-edible, especially the poisonous varieties if you want to survive this potentially lethal hobby. I find the names of the extremely poisonous mushrooms, such as the Destroying Angel, the Fly Agaric and Panther Cap, wonderfully sinister and mysterious, which is a good way of recalling their dangerous characteristics as well. I have only ever suffered once from eating wild mushrooms that I have collected and that was from a clump of Sulphur Tufts. It only gave us the runs so there was no real harm done and I believe this particular mushroom can frequently upset people's stomachs. An especially delicious dish is mushroom risotto finished off with a flourish of truffle oil. A rare and sought-after mushroom is the chanterelle, which we were lucky enough to discover in the French Alps near St Germain. Usually the only ones I have found in this country have been false chanterelle which are by no means the same. We were camping at the time but we feasted like lords on a mushroom omelette accompanied by a delicious local sauvignon blanc. The simple pleasures of life are the best.

I have always been adventurous when it comes to cooking and one of my earliest cookery books, which I still treasure, is Keith Floyd's 'Floyd on Fish '. One of his recipes I have used successfully is for bouillabaisse, the southern French speciality from Marseille. Many years ago I once had the opportunity of eating this at a harbour side restaurant in Marseille itself. I never forgot that experience and tried to recreate it, which I did to some extent but it is extremely difficult to do it justice unless one has absolutely freshly caught fish - not an easy thing to find in Shropshire. I am also the proud possessor of a traditional Austrian cookery book in German, which contains over 30 recipes for dumplings alone, savoury and sweet, filled and unfilled. I have made about five different kinds of what the Austrians call knodel so making and preparing food to me is not just a functional need for sustenance but the very stuff of life itself, combining as it does the reminiscences of far away cultures, creativity and sociability. I'm happy to say that my children have carried on this tradition, all of them enjoying cooking, eating and drinking well. We are a veritable family of foodies.

Languages

One of my passions in life, in addition to those I have already mentioned, is the learning of foreign languages. I think this could possibly be genetic because my father, whose schooling ended at 15 years of age, showed some proficiency and interest in learning languages during the war. As he went from Italy to France and finally into Germany, he picked up a smattering of these languages though I cannot say how proficient he was in them. At secondary school I recall being fascinated by the French language but, having a very poor teacher, made little progress in it and when I tried to use it the first time in France found that I could neither understand nor be understood. It was a most shameful and disappointing experience, which in later years I determined to rectify, which I did. I was lucky enough at school to be given the chance to study Latin and Greek, although without a great deal of success, but at least it provided a foundation for not only my use of English but also other modern European languages, particularly Spanish and Italian. Whenever I visit a country, I make it a rule to try and learn something of the language before I go, the exception being the Czech Republic where German is still widely spoken or at least understood. I therefore have a smattering of Portuguese and modern Greek in addition to the languages which I am much more fluent in i.e. French and German. Belatedly perhaps, about 10 years ago I also took an introductory course in Welsh on the Say Something in Welsh website, which was excellent. And, more recently, since I am no longer able to participate in an advanced French class, which I did until a year ago, I have undertaken to learn Arabic, which is a Semitic, not an Indo European language. Arabic script is quite challenging but one obtains a great deal of satisfaction from trying to decipher it and periodically I pick up the individual word on television news. But as none of my friends speak Arabic and it is very unlikely that I shall ever go to the Middle East now or any other Arabic speaking country, it is a purely academic exercise.

It was about 20 years ago I think when I was visiting friends in Austria and became dissatisfied when I couldn't always participate in the conversation because it was in German. My Austrian friends were much more comfortable with and keen to speak English and I had never learned German before. On one occasion, I remember, one of my friends said without any particular hostility: 'You should learn to speak German, after all you come here frequently enough. 'That spurred me on and I bought a Linguaphone package and a year or so later enrolled on German classes at the College where I worked, which I could do so free of charge. It was wonderfully satisfying to reach a level of fluency when I could deal with most situations and hold normal conversations with German speakers.

Learning a foreign language isn't always easy and unless you are particularly talented it is not something you can pick up in five minutes. It takes graft, application and hard work and for that you really should have a good reason for wanting to learn it. I have looked forward for years to when I retired and I could spend six months to a year in Salzburg, my favourite Austrian city, improving my German fluency. Sadly, this has not been possible. Whilst I was still working in my mid 50s, I looked for a German course to enrol on at one of the regional universities. I was hoping to take a part-time degree in German. However, there was nothing suitable which could be combined with full-time employment but I did settle eventually on an excellent course at Wolverhampton University, which would provide me with a certificate to teach English to foreign students. This was certificated by a Cambridge College and known as TESOL or teaching English to speakers of other languages. I had one mind on when I retired. This turned out to be a really excellent programme that taught me a lot I didn't know about my own language as well as whetting my appetite for linguistics. There was a reciprocal arrangement between the University and Telford College so I did not have to pay any fees. I thoroughly enjoyed the course and finished it with a top grade. Although I have not been able to use it in the way that I wanted, I found it extremely helpful in my own teaching of English to English speaking students so it wasn't wasted.

Chapter 15

Conclusion

What a rollercoaster of a journey since March 2017. That was the date of the Permissions hearing for the start of the legal case attempting to change the 1961 Suicide Act to allow assisted dying. Every foot of the way has been strongly contested by illiberal, traditional forces. Their ploy has been to set themselves up as the moral defenders of the weak and   vulnerable. They oppose every argument to allow the terminally ill to have their Article 8 rights respected i.e. the right to personal autonomy, the right to choose how and when they should die. The issue has been hotly debated throughout the land and hopefully will continue to be, whatever the outcome. It is clear that the vast majority of the

British public support my case and would want the same rights to be exercised in the event they were in similar circumstances.

I accept the sensitivity of the issue and of the need to provide obvious protections to those who are not in a position to express their own wishes. However, I have little sympathy with campaigners who hide behind a barrage of emotive rhetoric, distortion and outright misinformation, whose prime motivation lies in mediaeval ideology i.e. traditional religions and blind religious faith. In particular, I resent the power they have in our political institutions, a historical legacy, to block the wishes of the majority today. I know that not all religious people are so minded and the more liberal of them are compassionate supporting the case for change in order to alleviate unnecessary suffering. I'm still bemused by some of the non-sequiturs that have been displayed, even by one of the senior High Court Appeal judges, who claimed that by granting recognition of Article 8 rights to those who are terminally ill and within six months of death, would place unacceptable pressure on other terminally ill people who would not choose an assisted death. This is pure supposition for which there is no evidence and, given the safeguards for two doctors and a High Court judge to examine the motives of each applicant, I cannot see that this will be a problem. The latest information I have is that the Appeal Court judgement will be made by the end of court term, which means the end of July 2018. There will also be a judgement from the Supreme Court sometime soon in a case which pertains to the recognition of abortion in Northern Ireland but whose arguments also relate closely to Article 8 rights, and permission has been given for both appellant and defendant in my case to make additional submissions in the light of that ruling. My legal team are of the opinion that the appeal court will draw its own conclusions on the substantive arguments and not just endorse or refute the earlier Divisional Court ruling. So, the fight is not yet over legally and I hope that I have made some small contribution to extending Human Rights in the UK. It may well be true that none of this will be of any benefit to me and I will not be able to make use of an assisted death, but I'm sure some progress will have been made whatever the outcome and I do not regret the time and energy expended so far getting to where we are now.

So what lies ahead for me? The what is not in doubt but the when and the how remain unknown and a source of continual anxiety. Some might say if I could look forward to an afterlife, there would be no need to worry providing me with profound comfort in my final days. If I were to adopt such a position, it would be a betrayal of who I am and my basic values. I can remember as a child fixating on the person of Jesus, probably after some excursion to Sunday school, and developing an almost unhealthy devotion and faith in the Christian God. I'm not sure what my parents made of it because they were certainly not religious folk, but nor were they atheists or unbelievers. They just accepted it all, as most people did and probably still do, without taking it too seriously as it didn't really affect their lives. I can also remember vividly skipping down a rural lane on the outskirts of Falmouth, seeing and sniffing the surrounding flora as if for the first time. The sun was high and shafts of light shot through the branches above. It was good to be alive. But I had no awareness or consciousness of the divine at that time. It's curious how I remember that after all this time. When we returned to Lancashire, I remember joining the local church choir and attending services but none of the family did and when I progressed to a Church of England secondary school, I accepted worship and religious instruction as quite natural.

It was a few years later when I experienced what effectively was my own Reformation when I questioned the necessity of attending church or being led by the priest. Studying Marx and Feuerbach at university provided the intellectual framework which led ultimately to atheism. It was a deeply thought out position and I never went back on it. I admire David Hume who laid the foundations for the enlightenment version of atheism and whose life and death are an inspiration. When we die, we as individuals cease to exist and I have no problems with this, which is a scientifically rational position. There is no scientific basis for belief in divinities and I perceive the universe as a physical Cosmos in which humans are merely a collection of atoms and molecules which on death change form but can never be destroyed. There is no evidence at all for the continuation of human consciousness or, as some would say, the soul. I am a humanist and delight in the beauty of life and matter wherever it is.

It is claimed by some that at the end of life or, when one faces imminent death, that the whole of one's life unfolds before one in a rapid kaleidoscope of images and thoughts. I don't know whether that is the case or not, yet. However, it is certainly true that over the last three years I have had time and cause to reflect on the life I have had. Was it useful? What kind of a person was I? Was I 'successful'? Did I waste time or harm people? Was it all worthwhile? There are all manner of answers and responses that one can give to such questions and perhaps it is for others to do this. There are a number of observations I can make and I think at this moment in time I can honestly say whilst I have been blown around by the fortunes and misfortunes of life, like everyone else, ultimately it has been a good life. I was fortunate in having devoted and loving parents who stayed together and sacrificed everything for the children. My childhood memories, especially the early years, are positive ones and even later, through the turbulent teenage years, they were not unhappy. On reflection, I think my most difficult years were in my 20s when I was struggling to develop a fulfilling career, which I did, but at the same time was coping with separation and divorce with the potential loss of daily contact with my daughter. Had I got married later in life, how different might things have been? It is impossible to say. Nonetheless, I believe that I did come to know myself better and made choices that were my own so that I was able to make my own future, so far as that is possible for anyone. I did engage in politics, I did make a considerable difference to some people's lives i.e. students, which I believe was for the better, and I did choose my friends who have been a valuable and rewarding part of my life. The best decision I ever made was undoubtedly to make my life with Carol and to have a child with her, our son Alex. During these decades, which now seem to have flown by so quickly, I've always been self reflective and from time to time would consider what it was like to face imminent death. I know some people are not able to confront this question but I have. I'm sure that was one reason I became a humanist and also why later I drew up, as did Carol, an ADRT. It may have had something to do with the time when I was very young, probably about six or seven years of age, when an older cousin in response to the statement I must've made about living forever, 'No. You will die, everyone dies. 'It must have made a remarkable impact on me because I remember it to this day. I was mortified. But in those days, people answered such comments by saying that we would all go to heaven and live happily ever after. So death, the existential fear, according to psychologists, has not infested my subconscious or conscious with terror and demons. The only regret I do have is that I will not be able to share my retirement years with Carol and the family. I have been robbed of that by MND.

Now as I write this, three and 1/2 years after my diagnosis, when I cannot stand or walk, I feel as though I have become a stranger to my body. I look at my wasted forearms and remember the strength they gave me to pick my way up a vertical rock face or look for hidden holds with which to overcome the major challenge or crux of a difficult climb. Now they are not strong enough to raise my hands to my chin and soon I will not be able to move them at all. As I slouch in my rise and recline chair, I see the protruding mass of my stomach, as my muscles are too weak to hold in the ludicrous lengths of intestine. My feet have become swollen as immobility reduces circulation and oedema sets in. Is this really me? It is a far cry from the youth with the rippling stomach muscles, the young man with the hard biceps or the 60-year-old with a reasonably trim figure and powerful thighs who could cycle 30 miles with ease or run nimbly over Crib Goch scrambling fearlessly over the Needles in Snowdonia. I can no longer use a keyboard and it is only with great difficulty using the tip of one finger, on my Apple Mac Air touchpad along with the dictation facility, that I can write. I have returned the specially provided computer screen with the eye gaze technology that I loathed to use but kept just in case it was the only way to express myself. And I wonder how long it will be when I step over that line in the sand?

Recently, I received some new face masks, which allow me to talk more clearly even when I am using the NIV. This has improved my capacity for social intercourse, which is a fundamental requirement to remain human and has improved the balance a little. I now have to use my ventilator for 23 hours out of the 24 and in a few months it will no doubt be permanent. I still have my voice, unlike the vast majority of MND sufferers[35], and can still eat and drink almost without hindrance. But it is only a question of time before I lose these essential faculties and then what do I do? I have seen the press reports of those four poor Germans[36] in the final stages of MND frozen as if in cryogenic suspension enduring a suffering worse than hell itself. Even if my court case is successful and it is approved by Parliament, to legalise a limited form of assisted dying, it is unlikely to come soon enough to enable me to avoid this horror without having recourse to what I consider to be the equally unpalatable alternative of slowly suffocating to death, mitigated by the palliative provision of morphine and sedatives. I am currently enjoying a new lease of life with a new care team with whom I can talk genially and with one of them in German. I don't know when that time will come when I must make that final decision but come it must. My nights are increasingly disturbed and uncomfortable, which I may be able to alleviate by taking additional quantities of morphine. I wish I simply had the choice of asking someone to bring me the final life-ending dose of medication from the fridge when I am ready, but realistically that is not going to be possible. I will die a death I don't want in a way I don't want and for that I will not forgive the opponents of the change to the law which is sorely needed. Increasingly I resent the medical profession except for those, mainly younger ones, who believe in a truer

239

commitment to the Hippocratic oath with its recognition of patient autonomy. I look outside the window beside me and I see that finally the long, unseasonably cold winter and spring has ended and a warm summer promises to rekindle that love of life which the sun engenders. But for me there is little to rekindle and the hot days to come hold little welcome but the final arrival of that dark night.

June 2018

Post Script

It is now eight months later and I am still here to write a post script to the legal process that followed the disappointing Appeal Court decision in June 2018. In November 2018[37] a Permission application to the Supreme Court was rejected. This came as a bitter disappointment to all of those in the campaign group who had worked so tirelessly for two years to bring about change in UK law. Hopes had been riding high that we would at least obtain a hearing at the Supreme Court. Two of the High Court judges out of the three on the Permission panel had in the past declared their opinions in favour of change. The court expressed its sympathy for my case and recognised the legitimacy of the courts being able to make a judgement in such cases. However, from my point of view justice was not given a chance as the judgement was that my case had little chance of success at a full hearing of the Supreme Court. No judgement was made on the substance of the case. The outcome rested entirely on the opinion of whether success was likely or not. The Supreme Court therefore had no opportunity to listen to or debate the important issues of law that are central to the case. This appears to be an absolute denial of justice. Of course, even had our application been heard and judgement found in favour it would still be up to Parliament to decide whether to take it further. Now the Campaign must redouble its efforts to shift political opinion in Parliament, especially in the House of Commons where there was little support for change in 2015.

Considerable progress nonetheless has been made over the past two years. The issue itself has been widely discussed in the media and amongst the general population. Social media especially has played a large part in educating the public about the arguments. Other countries and legal jurisdictions have also come out in favour of assisted dying. It is now a case in the UK of not if, but when change will occur. Although for me the question of how my final days will be experienced has not been resolved, and I am still left with a profound anxiety about the process, I feel the effort and energy expended in the Campaign has not been in vain. One day, the United Kingdom will emerge from its mediaeval thraldom.

The End.
January 2019

..

Citation List

[1] R (N Conway) v Ministry of Justice 2017 UK
[2] Simon Nightingale (2017) BBC Radio Shropshire-thought for the day
http://www.bbc.co.uk/programmes/p04wtj7c#play
[3] Heart of Darkness (1899) by Joseph Conrad
[4] Crime and Punishment (1867) by Fyodor Dostoyevsky
[5] The will to power (1910) by Friedrich Nietzsche
[6] Motor Neurone Disease Association
[7] MND Research Blog (2018) Physical Activity and the Odds of Developing MND (24/4/18)
[8] MND Association: research: stem cell therapy(2017)
https://www.mndassociation.org/research/mnd-research-and-you/stem-cells/stem-cell-therapy/
[9] BBC News Magazine(2014)
http://www.bbc.co.uk/news/magazine-29013707
[10] MND Association (2017) Key facts and information about MND
[11] MSSociety.org.uk
[12] Huntingdon's disease Association at org.uk
[13] Association of British Neurologists survey of acute neurological services 2014
[14] " A Swiss based non profit organisation where people from any nation can obtain an assisted suicide in accordance with Swiss law Internet: www.dignitas.ch

[15] The campaign group in the UK which works to change the law so that it recognises assisted dying for certain groups of people and with whom I am working closely.: https://www.dignityindying.org.uk

[16] Populus (March 2015)

[17] British Medical Association Homepage (2017) https://www.bma.org.uk/advice/employment/ethics/ethics-a-to-z/physician-assisted-dying

[18] Care Not Killing in 2006 brought together 21 organisations to oppose any change to the law on assisted dying in the wake of Lord Joffre's bill.

[19] General Medical Council (2017) http://www.gmc-uk.org/guidance/ethical_guidance/end_of_life_disagreement_resolution.asp

[20] https://www.mydeath-mydecision.org.uk/info/options/double-effect-terminal-sedation/

[21] The blog Lloyd Riley (2017) Huffington Post: To Achieve Radical Change End-Of-Life Providers Need To Address Some Home Truths 23/05/2017 15:00 | Updated 24 May 2017

[22] Royal College of Physicians (2016)) National End of Life Care Audit – Dying in Hospital

[23] British Social Attitudes (2017) Euthanasia.

[24] The European Convention on Human Rights

[25] R(Conway) v Ministry of Justice [2017] UK

[26] R(Nicklinson) v Ministry of Justice [2014] UKSC 38

[27] Not Dead Yet UK, Care not Killing, Living and Dying Well

[28] Dignity in Dying (2015) Populus UK

[29] Not dead yet USA (2017) Not Dead Yet Disability Activists Oppose Assisted Suicide As A Deadly Form of Discrimination

Not Dead Yet UK (2017) Juliet Marlowe NOT DEAD YET UK STATEMENT ON MR NOEL CONWAY'S LEGAL CASE http://notdeadyetuk.org/mr-noel-conway-not-dead-yet-uk-statement/

[31] Appeal Court Judgement (2018) Case no. C1/2017/3068, para 19,The Senior President of Tribunals Lord Justice Underhill. (18/1/2018)

[32] equality human rights.com (accessed 22 April 2018)

[33] Human Rights Act (1998) Article 2 <www.legislation.gov.uk>

[34] Universal Declaration of Human Rights (1948) un.org

35

https://www.mndassociation.org/about-mnd/living-with-mnd/speech-and-communication/(accessed on 14 July 2017)

[36] Completely 'locked-in' patients can communicate. BBC News, February 1 2017.

[37] Hearing for Permission to appeal to the Supreme Court, 27th of November 2018 before Lady Hale, Lord Kerr, and Lord Reed.

Printed in Poland
by Amazon Fulfillment
Poland Sp. z o.o., Wrocław